DECORATIVE IRONWORK

DECORATIVE IRONWORK

Marian Campbell

V&A Publications

For my parents

First published by V&A Publications, 1997

V&A Publications
160 Brompton Road, London SW3 1HW

© The Board of Trustees of the Victoria and Albert Museum 1997

Marian Campbell asserts her moral right to be identified as the author of this book

Designed by Bernard Higton

ISBN 1 85177 195 6

A catalogue record for this book is available from the British Library

Printed in Hong Kong by South Sea International

The V&A is most grateful to the Worshipful Company of Armourers and
Brasiers (Gauntlet Trust) and the Worshipful Company of Ironmongers for
their generous grants which allowed the inclusion of more and better
photographs than would otherwise have been possible

*Note: In general all illustrations are the property and copyright of the V&A.
Where they are not, their source is stated in the caption and the copyright holder
credited accordingly in brackets*

Front of jacket: Locksmith's sign; wrought iron. German, late eighteenth
century. 545-1869.
Back of jacket: Cockerel; iron and copper, embossed and painted. French, early
eighteenth century. Perhaps from an inn-sign or weather-vane. 909-1906.
Half-title page: Door-knocker; wrought iron. French, seventeenth century. 1219-1855.
Frontispiece: Blackfriars Bridge, over the Thames, London; designed by
Joseph Cubitt, 1863-9. The arches are of cast and wrought iron, with a cast iron
cornice and parapet. Largely demolished in the 1950s. (John Gay.)
Contents page: Dragon; articulated, wrought iron with gilt eyes and copper tongue.
Signed Myôchin Nobumasa. Japanese, nineteenth century. M 37-1947.

CONTENTS

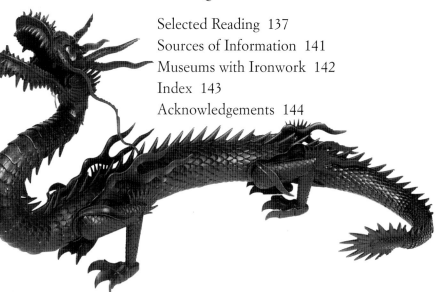

INTRODUCTION

To a twentieth-century eye used to the severe functionalism of contemporary iron security grilles and crowd crush-barriers, the beauty and versatility of historic ironwork come as a surprise. Yet much ironwork, both wrought and cast, consists of bold patterns and linear designs of graphic power and aesthetic appeal. The inherent strength of iron has long made it ideal for security purposes – for the protection of doors by elaborate hinges and locks, of windows by ornate grilles and of property by gates and railings. Its decorative qualities have attracted architects to use it for balconies and staircases, for bridges and even for entire buildings. In the domestic sphere, from early times until about 1900, wrought or cast iron played an important part in the vital activities of cooking, lighting and heating.

When displayed in museums, ironwork can be studied closely, but it suffers the disadvantage of being divorced from its original setting and, too often, stripped of its colours. By illustrating the context as well as the detail of a subject large in scope as well as scale, it is hoped that this brief overview – drawing extensively on the V&A collections – will show the great versatility of the metal.

———

Iron, when associated with other elements, is one of the most plentiful metals on earth, but is neither extracted nor worked with ease. In Europe, until the late Middle Ages, the only known method of working iron was for a blacksmith to shape it by hammering it in a forge, to produce wrought iron. No two pieces of wrought iron will ever be identical.

With technological advances around 1400, it became possible to melt iron into liquid form. This, when poured into moulds, produced cast iron, and allowed the mass-production of identical objects. By the early nineteenth century cast iron had become the dominant form of the worked metal, and was so easily and cheaply available that it was used and misused in superabundance. As a result, iron today is all too rarely associated with beauty.

The natural characteristics of wrought and cast iron are very different, and the techniques used in making both have always exerted a controlling influence on their design. Wrought iron readily lends itself to elegantly symmetrical forms, and is highly suitable for gates, balconies and balustrades, candlesticks or trivets. Cast iron, on the other hand, is better employed for repeating patterns, such as railing uprights, and for designs in relief, like firebacks. Being more fire-resistant than wrought iron, cast iron is the more suitable for firegrates. The visual appearance of much ironwork was originally often enhanced by colours and by gilding — gates, staircases and chandeliers were rarely the sober black so common today.

It is frequently difficult to be precise about the date or the attribution of ironwork. Smiths were often conservative and continued working in styles whose fashion had long since waned. Little is known of the identities or lives of more than a handful of smiths, and most work is unsigned and very rarely marked. With cast iron, the replication inherent in the manufacturing process makes it almost impossible to establish the date of the metal (as distinct from that of its pattern). However, attribution is aided, in the case of nineteenth-century pieces, by the intense, competitive pride of the foundries, which cast their names into lamp-posts, pillar-boxes, benches and railings.

1. Gates at Chatsworth House, Derbyshire; wrought iron, embossed and gilt, possibly made by the smith Richard Oddy, c. 1720, but placed in their present position only about 1829.

THE V&A COLLECTION AND ITS CONTEXT

The Ironwork Gallery of the Victoria & Albert Museum remains as much a place of fascination today as when described in 1900 by H.G. Wells, in his novel *Love and Mr Lewisham*:

> 'As one goes into the South Kensington Art Museum from the Brompton Road, the Gallery of Old Iron is overhead to the right. But the way thither is exceedingly devious and not to be revealed to everybody, since the young people ... set a peculiar value on its seclusion. The gallery is long and narrow and dark, and set with iron gates, iron-bound chests, locks, bolts and bars, fantastic great keys, lamps, and the like, and over the balustrade one may lean and talk of one's finer feelings.'

The V&A holds the British national collection of ironwork, the most comprehensive such collection in the world. As a result the museum is the one place where the history and development of styles and forms of ironwork from Britain and continental Europe can be studied as an integrated whole. The collection numbers some 2,000 items, mainly of European origin but with a few choice pieces from North America, Japan and India. It is diverse, ranging from objects of domestic and architectural use – furniture, firegrates and gates, locks and keys, chests and candlesticks – to the unexpected, in the form of jewellery.

Much of the collection was acquired between about 1850 and 1920, as a result of the widespread demolition and alteration of old buildings in Europe during this time; if not thrown away, iron fittings were often sold off as scrap metal. Although there is a good collection of cast iron firebacks and firedogs, the principal glory of the collection is its wrought iron, especially dating from about 1600 to 1800, the result of a deliberate museum policy in the nineteenth century. From its very foundation the museum pioneered the collection of 'old iron' – the earliest such purchase was a pair of wrought iron seven-teenth-century German hinges in 1844. It did not collect cast iron, although, paradoxically, the early museum buildings themselves incorporated a good deal of ironwork, predominantly cast, some of which is still in place.

Made of corrugated sheet iron in 1856, the predecessor of the present building was nicknamed 'the Brompton Boilers'. The great South Court, richly stencilled and coloured, designed by the Sheffield artist and designer Godfrey Sykes (1825–66; fig. 3), were praised at their opening in 1862: 'the way in which wrought and cast iron is deployed in them is particularly worthy of study ... the constant change in the coloured ornament ... preserves the entire design from ... monotony which the extensive use of cast iron often leads to' (*Building News*, 14 February 1865). As the galleries are now used for temporary exhibitions all this is currently covered over with plasterboard, but other ironwork is visible, such as the cresting, ornamented with winged dragons, on the outside of the Lecture Theatre roof. Also designed by Sykes, it was cast in 1868 by the London metalworkers Hart & Son, and cost £385, less than half the price estimated for wrought iron. Inside, the screen at the head of the Lecture Theatre stairs (fig. 4), as well as the balusters, were again designed by Sykes, modelled by architect James Gamble (1835–1911) and cast by Smith & Co. of London in 1868. All were originally coloured with a special bronze paint invented by a Frenchman, L. Oudry. The museum's original restaurant was supplied with a decorative cast iron grill and ovens to the designs of Sir Edward Poynter (1836–1919), artist and designer and from 1875 to 1893 Director for Art at the museum, and cast by Hart & Son in 1868 for £165 (fig. 7).

2 (above). Gutter-spout; cast iron by Thomas Elsley of London, 1905.

3. The South Courts (1862–5) of the V&A soon after completion, looking north; the arcade is of wrought and cast iron and the floor grilles of cast iron. Photographed by J. Davis Burton in 1868.

4. V&A Lecture Theatre screen: detail showing a child holding the lamp of learning; cast iron by Smith & Co., London, 1868.

5. Lecture by Mr Capes on the Ironwork Collection, in the museum in 1870. Engraving from the *Illustrated London News*.

6 (opposite). Gates to the V&A Science Entrance in Exhibition Road; wrought iron, English, by J. Starkie Gardner & Co., 1886. Seen here from the back, the gates incorporate the monogram 'SKM', for South Kensington Museum, the name by which the museum was known until 1899.

7. Grill in the 'Dutch Kitchen' at the V&A; cast iron and brass. English, designed by Sir Edward Poynter, dated 1868 and made by Hart & Son. The 'Dutch Kitchen' was one of three dining rooms which made up the old restaurant, and was in use, along with the grill, until 1939.

Little survives of the cast iron furniture designed for the museum by the famous sculptor Alfred Stevens (1817–75). Restaurant tables to his design were cast in 1868 by Stevens & Hoole of Sheffield. The comment of a contemporary in *The Standard* of the same year, that 'they have a good effect but are almost miraculously small', probably explains their subsequent removal – just two exist today. Stevens's other commission was for the massive cast radiator grilles or 'coil-cases', also by Hoole, which were installed in 1866 and dismantled in the 1940s.

Wrought iron came late to the building. Gates to what was then the museum mews, now the Science Gate, were designed in 1886 by John Starkie Gardner (the well-known writer on ironwork; 1844–1930) and made by his Lambeth firm of metalworkers, Starkie Gardner & Co., who were in business until 1994 (fig. 6). A century later came the commissions to Jim Horrobin (b. 1946) for gates to the Ironwork Gallery (1981; fig. 220), and to the American metal sculptor Albert Paley (b. 1944) for an iron bench for it (1994; fig. 32).

PART ONE

BRIEF HISTORY

EARLY HISTORY AND THE MIDDLE AGES

The early history of iron working has been obscured by the paradoxical nature of the metal: strong, yet prone to rust. Unprotected iron objects will rust away and decay entirely in a very few years. As a result there are few remnants of the products of the blacksmiths of antiquity, which were probably predominantly weapons and tools.

Some iron beads of *c.* 3500 BC, found at Jirzah in Egypt, appear to be among the earliest known wrought iron artefacts, but they are made of meteoric iron. Also of meteoric iron is the sword of Tutankhamun (*c.* 1360 BC; Cairo Museum, Egypt), found in his gold coffin, which was probably a treasured possession and perhaps a gift from a ruler of one of the ironworking districts of Asia Minor. The technique of extracting iron from the ore seems to have been mastered by 2800 BC, the date

8. The Capel Garmon firedog; wrought iron, Celtic, *c.* 50 BC–AD 50. Found in a peat bog in Denbigh in 1852. Cardiff, National Museum of Wales. (National Museum of Wales.)

ascribed to fragments of a wrought iron dagger blade found at Tall al-Asmar in Mesopotamia. However, the first real iron industry was probably not established until between about 2000 and 1500 BC in Asia Minor. The knowledge of iron production and working spread slowly from the Middle East westwards to Greece, probably by about 1000 BC, and so to the rest of Europe, reaching the British Isles around 500 BC. The Chinese were, from at least the sixth century AD, skilled in the production of cast iron, which was not known in the West until the late Middle Ages, but they apparently did not make wrought iron. This may well indicate that their discovery of the metal was entirely independent and not the result of Western influence.

Iron seems at first to have been rare, and consequently perhaps considered to have semi-magical powers. Once it had become comparatively easy to obtain it appears to have been used not only for weapons and tools but for everyday items. A number of Celtic firedogs survive from northern Europe, such as one from the first century AD (fig. 8) in the National Museum of Wales, Cardiff. Like several others, it is dramatically decorated with elaborate terminals in the shape of horses' heads. The Romans, on the other hand, appear to have used decorative wrought iron sparingly. Iron rings were given as tokens of engagement in the first century AD, according to Pliny; iron window-grilles are known from both Pompeii and Herculaneum, as well as from British sites such as the Roman villa of Hinton St Mary, Dorset (now in the British Museum, fig. 33). Complex decorative ironwork is not generally found before the Middle Ages, probably because it was not made, but possibly because it has perished. Perhaps more typical of the early medieval period is the practical but intricate cauldron suspension

9. Doors from Gannat, Auvergne; wrought iron on wood. French, thirteenth century. M 396-1924.

medieval doors and chests with elaborate ironwork, many still in the places for which they were made. Some of the most intricate stamped scrollwork hinges ever made are those designed for Notre Dame Cathedral in Paris in the thirteenth century. Although nineteenth-century copies now ornament the doors, parts of the originals are preserved in the Musée de Cluny, Paris.

Grilles might be very simple, like the thirteenth-century examples still in Canterbury and Lincoln Cathedrals – consisting of back-to-back C scrolls held together by 'collars' – or might be rather more varied, like the screens from Salisbury Cathedral still *in situ*. Complex designs, transformed from the scrolling motif into flower terminals, can be found on thirteenth-century grilles, as in those in the Musée le Secq des Tournelles in Rouen, in Winchester Cathedral (from St Swithun's shrine), or still *in situ* in various French and Belgian churches. A famous and elaborate example of stamped scrollwork is the grille which still guards the tomb of Eleanor of Castile (d. 1296) in Westminster Abbey (fig. 193). This has the rare added distinction of being by a known maker, Thomas de Leghtune (from Leighton Buzzard, Bucks; fl. 1280s–90s), who, according to the royal accounts, was paid £13 for making, transporting and installing the grille.

Another much used motif was the quatrefoil (cluster of four petals), found in screens and grilles all over Europe; rare dated examples can be seen in Italy, in Orvieto Cathedral (1337), Santa Croce in Florence (1371) and the Palazzo Pubblico, Siena (1436; fig.11). Floral or leaf-shaped terminals cut from sheet iron, as at Siena, appear to have been in use as early as the thirteenth century in Germany: gates so decorated can be seen in Hildesheim Cathedral. Commonplace by the fifteenth century, the motif of cut-out leaves continued well into the sixteenth century, often decorating the tops of tomb railings and screens.

In the fifteenth century blacksmiths began imitating the designs that were then being produced by their contemporaries, with rather more ease, in wood and stone. This necessitated carving the iron when cold, a laborious and difficult technique. The gates still in place around the chantry of Henry V (d. 1422) in Westminster Abbey, London, demonstrate the remarkable three-dimensional effect that could be achieved by overlaying complex geometrical motifs. Their maker was the King's blacksmith, Roger Johnson. Later, in *c.*1483, another royal blacksmith, John Tresilian, made the screen and gates for Edward IV's chantry chapel in the same difficult tech-

chain, dating to the seventh century, found at Sutton Hoo, Suffolk (British Museum). It is made up of plain loops which interlock with others shaped as the horns of stylized rams' heads.

One of the commonest medieval uses of ironwork was for the protection of wooden doors and chests. All needed strengthening, and so elaborate hinges were designed to cover much of the surface and act as both hinge and guard. One of the earliest pieces in the V&A is the twelfth-century hinge-work saved in the 1880s from the then semi-derelict St Alban's Abbey (fig. 10); the hinges are decorated with S-shaped scrolls, an elaboration upon the C shapes that are more common at this date. More angular motifs can be seen on the thirteenth-century doors from Gannat in France (fig. 9). Hinge scrollwork could be extremely elaborate, and was often stamped with dies of different patterns, as on a late thirteenth-century door at Merton College, Oxford. England and Scandinavia are particularly rich in surviving

10 (above). Hinge from the slype door of St Alban's Abbey, Herts; wrought iron, engraved, twelfth century. Discarded during the radical alterations of the 1880s. 359-1889.

11 (right). Chapel screen in the Palazzo Pubblico, Siena: detail; wrought iron. Italian, by Niccolò di Paolo, 1436. The cut-out cresting and elaborate quatrefoil motifs are characteristic at this date. The frieze includes scenes of Romulus and Remus suckled by the wolf.

nique, closely imitating contemporary stone and wood carving; though now devoid of their original gilding, they are still in place in St George's Chapel, Windsor.

Iron was especially suitable for strengthening doors and encasing their locks, which were used from an early date. Locksmithing was always a skilled and specialist side of the blacksmiths' craft which required cold cutting of the iron and great precision. The collections of the V&A and of the Musée le Secq des Tournelles in Rouen, France, are rich in ornate locks and keys from doors and chests from all over Europe. One of the most elaborate locks still boasts its original gilding (fig. 12) and is entirely Gothic in style, for all that it was made for King Henry VIII (r. 1509–47), a patron of Renaissance styles. It came originally from a royal manor, Beddington Place in Surrey, and is probably by the locksmith who worked for the King from at least 1514, Henry Romayn (d. 1553).

Iron was important for chests and coffers, which from the Middle Ages to the eighteenth century were the principal means of safeguarding valuables – clothes, plate, jewellery or books. Sir Thomas Bodley's chest (Divinity School, Oxford) was given by Bodley (1545–1613) to his Library to hold its property deeds and coin. The chest is painted with his arms and those of the University and is today used for visitors' donations.

In architecture, iron had for a long time a functional purpose, to join or support timber and masonry, but apart from screens and gates, which were both decorative and yet integral to a building, it was not widely used in the visible architecture of the early Middle Ages. Such features as iron balconies seem only to appear in the fourteenth century, first perhaps in Italy. An early example, now in the Birmingham Museum and Art Gallery, comes from the Venetian palace of Casa Bartolomeo. Decorative minor architectural fittings were also being made in fourteenth-century Italy: lantern holders, dog-nosed wall-brackets and hooks, door-knobs and handles, which can still be seen on the walls of houses in Siena and Florence.

From an early date, some domestic items were usually made in iron – candlesticks and more rarely chandeliers – but iron was more vitally connected with the fireplace and with cooking. Firedogs and firebacks, cauldrons, spits, trivets and chimney cranes were all made of iron, and were often decorative as well as efficient. Most surviving examples are impossible to date with certainty or precision; for instance, the wrought iron firedog shown in fig. 108 is of Gothic design but very probably dates from the seventeenth century. Almost no examples of the spits and cauldrons depicted in medieval manuscripts survive, but they probably differed little in design from their eighteenth-century counterparts.

The introduction of cast iron was the great innovation in the late Middle Ages. Early guns and cannon like Mons Meg in Edinburgh Castle (Flemish, *c.* 1440) were usually made by the laborious process of welding together wrought iron bars. Expensive cast bronze was in use by *c.* 1400, but was superseded by cheaper cast iron, first used in Europe around 1400 for military purposes. One of the earliest surviving cast iron cannons (*c.* 1400) is the Bodiam mortar (at Bodiam Castle, Sussex).

At first it was probably only as a sideline that the foundries producing cannon also made firedogs and firebacks. These were also an innovation in the fifteenth century, when fireplaces with chimneys had only recently come into fashion.

12. The Beddington lock; iron, wrought, carved and gilded. English, probably made by Henry Romayn, *c.* 1539–52. It was originally on the main door to the great hall of Beddington Place, Surrey, held by the Crown 1539–52. The arms are those used by all Tudor monarchs, beginning with Henry VII. Henry Romayn was a blacksmith and held the post of lockmaker to Henry VIII and Edward VI. M 397-1921.

THE SIXTEENTH AND SEVENTEENTH CENTURIES

Even in the sixteenth and seventeenth centuries, when Renaissance ideas and styles were often adopted by metalworkers, much ironwork continued to be made according to the earlier fashion. The V&A has an outstanding collection of firebacks from these centuries, in which English examples predominate. They are often said to have all been made in the Weald in Sussex, an important ironworking centre since Roman times. However other parts of the country, notably the Forest of Dean in Gloucestershire, had just as ancient reputations for the production and working of iron, and it is likely that many firebacks should rather be attributed there.

Political themes were popular on seventeenth-century English and continental firebacks. One example depicts an oak and the initials 'CR' and probably commemorates Charles II's famous escape after the Battle of Worcester in 1651 during the Civil War by hiding in an oak tree. A Flemish example illustrates the struggle of the Spanish Netherlands to gain independence (1567–1609; fig. 112). From the sixteenth century onwards in cold northern Europe, especially in Germany and Scandinavia, free-standing cast iron stoves were popular, often being composed of three or four tiers, made up of several stove-plates riveted together. These, like firebacks, tended to portray a moralizing theme and often depict biblical scenes (fig. 119). Firedogs were made all over Europe in cast iron, as well as wrought iron, which it had largely superseded by the seventeenth century. This was no doubt

14. 'Armada' fireback; cast iron. English, perhaps Sussex, 1588. Its date coincides with the defeat of the Spanish Armada; the initials 'IFC' are those of its owner rather than its maker. Modern reproductions of the design are common. M 77-1957.

partly because cast iron was cheaper to produce, and partly because the fire-resistant qualities of cast iron were greater than those of wrought iron.

Renaissance motifs, even in Italy, were slow to find their way into the blacksmiths' repertoire, in which the Gothic style survived well into the sixteenth century. However the simple elegance of a pair of Italian sixteenth-century window-grilles in the V&A is in shape and style undoubtedly post-Gothic, as are the ebulliently Baroque embossed figures on a seventeenth-century staircase balustrade, also Italian (fig. 64). This would no doubt originally have been brightly painted and gilt, rather like the ornate Spanish

13 (opposite). *Reja* to the Constable's Chapel at Burgos Cathedral, Spain; wrought iron, embossed and carved, by Cristobal Andino. Spanish, 1523, in the *plateresco* style characteristic of Spanish Renaissance ironwork. Most unusually, the smith has signed his work, 'AB ANDINO' ('by Andino'), visible between the kneeling figures at the top. Photographed by Professor J.H. Weaver.

15 (below). Panel from a screen; iron, embossed and painted. Spanish, sixteenth century. M 97-1914.

panels (fig. 15) of the sixteenth century. Known by the Spanish as *plateresco* (that is, 'in the manner of a silversmith'), the technique – one undoubtedly more suited to metals softer than iron – demanded great skill. The Spanish were prodigious users of decorative ironwork from at least the fifteenth century and were unsurpassed in the sixteenth century. Huge *rejas* (screens) from this period still adorn many Spanish churches and cathedrals, as in Barcelona, Burgos (fig. 13), Seville and Granada. Some are as much as 30 feet (9 metres) high, and they are often embellished with colour, gilding and silvering. These screens usually incorporate balusters skilfully decorated by means of cold carving, which despite its difficulty was also a popular technique with Spanish smiths. Large portions of *rejas* from Avila Cathedral are in the V&A, and date from the late fifteenth to the sixteenth century. In New York the Metropolitan Museum houses the vast eighteenth-century *reja* (also 30 ft or 9 m high) from Valladolid Cathedral, removed earlier this century because changes in liturgical practice meant that it was causing an obstruction.

The versatility of smiths in Italy in the seventeenth century is demonstrated in screens and grilles in which ribbon-like iron strips, or round or square-sectioned bars, are used characteristically to very different effect (figs 35 and 38). Extremely rare oddities in the V&A are two Venetian gondola irons of the seventeenth century, engraved and wrought (fig. 19). Although gondolas today have simple, standardized iron prows (fig.18), the use of iron for their elaborate prows and sometimes sterns has

a long history. They evolved as a type of boat suited to the calm, shallow waters of the Venetian lagoon. As early as the fifteenth century, depictions exist of their elaborate prows, descendants perhaps of the exotic animal-headed prows represented on the ships in the Bayeux Tapestry. Visiting Venice in 1645, the diarist John Evelyn (1620–1706) noted the elaborate iron gondola prows. In the eighteenth century, many of Canaletto's paintings (fig. 17) show highly decorated gondolas of different styles. Some just have an elaborate prow, others have both elaborate prow and stern irons. The design of the seventeenth-century V&A gondola irons, with their intricate floral decoration and scrolling form, is strikingly similar to that of the stern irons on Canaletto's gondolas.

North of the Alps blacksmithing at this date showed equal skill, though the style was very different. A heavy Flemish window-grille of the early sixteenth century (now V&A) from the chapel of the Gravensteen, the Castle of the Counts of Flanders in Ghent, is largely Gothic, consisting of massive spiked iron bars decorated with somewhat incongruous dog-like terminals. The design of a seventeenth-century German lunette (fig. 16) seems, by contrast, whimsically decorative. The use of round-sectioned bars, the trick of threading one bar

17 (opposite top). *The Basin of San Marco on Ascension Day*; oil painting by Giovanni Antonio Canal, called Canaletto (1697–1768). National Gallery, London. (National Gallery.)

18 (opposite bottom left). Gondola prow and rowlock; steel. Venetian, twentieth century. Photographed by Edwin Smith. PH 852-1987. (Edwin Smith.)

19 (opposite bottom right). Gondola iron; steel, engraved. Italian, seventeenth century. 345-1880.

16. Lunette; wrought iron. German, seventeenth century. 1176-1864.

through another and the scrolling design are marked characteristics of German blacksmithing of this period and right into the nineteenth century.

In southern Germany and Switzerland, wrought iron was sometimes fashioned to create the effect of architectural perspective in huge church screens by means of piercing sheet iron to a pattern of receding columns, as in the V&A's screen from Constance Cathedral in Switzerland (fig. 20). Probably by the blacksmith Johann Reifell (fl. 1640s), it dates from c.1646 and, though it is now black, underlying paint layers show that it was originally painted in light blue and gold. Many such screens are still in place, for example in the cathedrals of Lucerne and Zürich and in the abbey churches of Muri and Einsiedeln (fig. 190) in Switzerland and in Germany in the church of Sts Ulrich and Afra, Augsburg, while others have been transplanted; there is one in the gardens at Powerscourt, Co. Wicklow, Ireland. Also characteristic of southern German blacksmiths' work of this period are elaborate and whimsical gutter spouts, of which the V&A possesses an example of a dragon and a devil (fig. 21), as well as intricately worked grave crosses (fig. 204).

20. Screen; wrought iron, by Johann Reifell, c. 1646. Swiss, from Constance Cathedral, Switzerland. 57-1890.

The specialist skill of locksmithing is demonstrated in many outstanding German examples, the most elaborate of which is in the so-called iron 'Armada' chest (fig. 183), where the lock mechanism entirely covers the inside lid. Many such chests, produced particularly in Nuremberg from c.1600 to 1800, were exported all over Europe. An early example is the chest bequeathed to the Bodleian Library, Oxford, by its founder Sir Thomas Bodley.

The Gothic style long persisted in France; little or no large-scale architectural ironwork was produced until the seventeenth century. However a school of locksmithing grew up under the patronage of Francis I (d. 1547) and Henry II (d. 1559), which produced highly complex locks, keys and caskets in the Renaissance style in brilliantly polished chiselled iron. Among these is the famous 'Strozzi' key (fig. 22), which is alleged to have been made to allow Diane de Poitiers, Henry II's mistress, entry to the King's private apartments. The bow – the loop forming the handle – is made up of two grotesque figures back-to-back, a design typical of many French keys. The superb gates of c.1642 to the Galerie d'Apollon in the Louvre were made originally for the chateau of Maisons-sur-Seine; they were perhaps designed by Jean Marot

(1619–79) they are technically close to locksmithing, being made of polished chiselled steel.

A renaissance in architectural iron-work was encouraged by Louis XIII, whose reign began in 1610; he was himself an amateur blacksmith who had forges installed at his palaces of the Tuileries and Fontainebleau for the royal blacksmith Rossignol. For the rest of the seventeenth century the craft blossomed in France, responding to a need for ironwork for the numerous newly built mansions and palaces, parks and gardens. Among many famous ironwork designers were Jean Bérain (1637–1711), Daniel Marot (1663–1752) and Jean Le Pautre (1618–82); characteristic of all is a fondness for symmetrical scrollwork with *repoussé* embellishments and the use of square-sectioned bars riveted together. Work of this period can best be seen *in situ*: at Chantilly, Fontainebleau, St Cloud and, above all, at Versailles. Here the century's most notable work was made for Louis XIV (r. 1643–1715). The bevy of smiths employed included Luchet for the entrance gates and railings (1678–9; fig. 81) and Nicolas Delobel for the balconies in the Cour de Marbre (1679–90) and the Escalier du Roi (1677–83).

In England the shrugging off of a Gothic style was equally hesitant. The gates of 1525–33 to Bishop West's chantry chapel in Ely Cathedral show a lingering fondness for the Gothic in their ogee arches, although coupled with an attempt at a naturalistic floral design that is more Renaissance in spirit. Similar motifs decorate chandelier suspension-rods, such as seventeenth-century examples in the V&A (fig. 147), where three-

dimensional design is enhanced by the remarkable survival of original colour and gilding. At the end of the seventeenth century the gates and window-grilles below the Wren Library in Trinity College, Cambridge, by William Partridge (fig. 37), retain vestiges of this floral motif combined more prominently with symmetrical C scrolls of classic simplicity, which herald much of the wrought ironwork in England of the eighteenth century.

By contrast comes the lush exuberance of the work of Jean Tijou (fl. 1689–1712), who is renowned above all for the numerous screens and gates he made for his royal patrons, William and Mary, for the Fountain Garden at Hampton Court, near London. Made between 1689 and 1696, they cost £2,160 2s. 0¼d, including the iron and workmanship, a fabulous sum at the time. Most can still be seen at Hampton Court, while a number of fragments are on loan to the V&A (fig. 23). Tijou is a somewhat mysterious figure, a Protestant Frenchman who left France after the revocation of the Edict of Nantes in 1685, was in England by about 1687 and left around 1712, at which point records of him cease. Other examples of his work can be seen in place at Burghley House, Stamford, and in the form of screens in St Paul's Cathedral, London. All make much use of *repoussé* work, the first instance of this technique in iron in England. Tijou was however a lone star, and left no real successors, although later generations of English smiths employed some of the *repoussé* motifs he had introduced.

Celia Fiennes (1662–1741), who in her travels around England in the late seventeenth century provided a comprehensive survey of the country, particularly noticed ironwork. Of Burghley House, Stamford, she wrote: 'the door on top of the Stepps is of iron carv'd, the finest I ever saw, all sorts of leaves, flowers, figures, birds, beast, wheat, in the Carving; very large the doors are' (*Journeys of Celia Fiennes*, ed. C. Morris, 1947).

21 (above). Gutter spout; iron, embossed and painted. German, seventeenth century. 1210-1872.

22 (left). 'Strozzi' key; steel, chiselled. French, late sixteenth or early seventeenth century; engraving. It is supposedly the key of Diane de Poitiers, but probably dates from slightly later; an engraving of a similar key is in *La Fidelle ouverture de l'art du Serrurier*, the locksmithing treatise published in 1627 in Paris. M 137-1927.

23 (right). Mask from the Fountain Garden Screen, Hampton Court; wrought iron, embossed. English, by Jean Tijou, c. 1693. On loan to the V&A from Historic Royal Palaces.

21

THE EIGHTEENTH CENTURY

All over Europe, the eighteenth century was a golden age for blacksmiths, whose skills created the screens and gates for parks, grand staircases and balconies for the increasing numbers of houses of the newly prosperous. Much of their work is still in place – in England, particularly in Oxford and Cambridge – but little retains its original gilding and colour, which would have been dark blue, grey, green or white. Throughout the century the design of English wrought iron was a restrained blend of symmetrical motifs, of uprights, water-leaves (V- or W-shaped leaves with crimped edges) and C scrolls. The embossed work of Tijou was not practised on so luxuriant a scale by his successors, though the fine early eighteenth-century work of Robert Bakewell (fl. 1707–52), as at Melbourne Hall, Derbys (fig. 24), and of the Davies family of smiths of Wrexham, at the 'White Gates' at Leeswood Hall, near Mold, north Wales (fig. 80), shows a distinctive tempering with embossed motifs of the Classical repertoire of uprights and C scrolls.

Elsewhere in Europe native styles of ironwork continued to flourish. In German-speaking areas, blacksmiths' work is found in abundance, notable for a continuing use of elaborate foliage and interlaced bars, the curving forms of which flow with extraordinary plasticity, especially in gates and screens. However the most exciting innovation of the century was the riotous symmetry and asymmetry of the Rococo style, conceived in France in the 1720s, exemplified by the choir screens in Amiens Cathedral designed by Gabriel Huquier (1695–1772). French and German blacksmiths were inspired to produce in iron marvellous and paradoxically lightweight effects, undoubtedly enhanced originally by colour and gilding.

The Rococo was scarcely adopted by British smiths. French work in this style can best be seen *in situ*, as in the gates and screens by Jean Lamour (1698–1771) in the Place Stanislas in Nancy (fig. 26). One of the few French examples in the V&A is the balcony of *c.*1770 from a house in Versailles. This is decorated with baskets of fruit

and flowers, and bears the arms of the blacksmiths' guild of Paris as its central motif – most aptly, for the probable maker, and owner of the house, was Jean François Cahon, royal blacksmith to Louis XVI (r.1774–93).

Towards the end of the eighteenth century the revival of the Classical style brought an elegance and restraint to the design of ironwork. A building boom in cities all over Europe coincided with the new availability of cast iron. It was suitable, in a way that wrought iron never could be, for casting with the fashionable Neo-classical motifs, and it was much cheaper because of newly improved production methods. In England cast iron had first been used architecturally, for railings, early in the century. These show in their size and shape a debt to the design of cannon, which formed the principal products of the iron foundries of the day. The earliest cast iron railings are those around St Paul's Cathedral in London (*c.*1714), made in Lamberhurst, Kent. Sections removed when the railings were resited earlier this century can be seen in

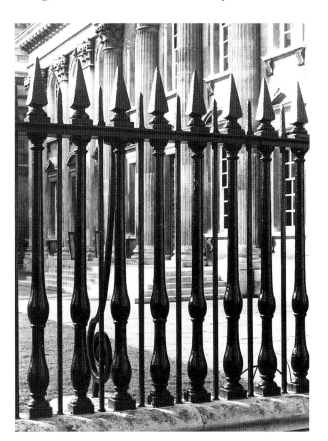

24 (opposite). The Arbour; wrought and embossed iron, at Melbourne Hall, Derbys, made by Robert Bakewell, 1707-11, and one of his earliest and most skilful works. (A.F. Kersting.)

25 (right). Railings outside the Senate House, Cambridge. English, *c.*1730. The large uprights are of cast iron, the slender ones wrought. (Author.)

English collections (the V&A, Hastings Museum and Anne of Cleves House, Lewes) and as far afield as Canada (High Park, Toronto). Other early cast iron railings still surround the Senate House, Cambridge (*c.* 1730; fig. 25) and St Martin-in-the-Fields, London (1726), designed by the architect James Gibbs (1718–80).

Later that century the influential writer Isaac Ware would recommend the use of cast iron in his book *The Complete Body of Architecture* (1756), and from the 1770s the cast iron industry began to flourish in Britain. Abraham Darby III (1750–91), of the Coalbrookdale Foundry in Shropshire, cast the first iron bridge in the world in 1779, to span the local river, the Severn. The family foundry established itself as producer of a wide range of gates, grates and stoves and, later on, furniture. In Scotland the Carron Ironworks in Stirlingshire specialized in the late eighteenth century in producing graceful

Neo-classical balconies and balusters, stoves and fireplaces, all designed by the architect brothers Robert (1728–92) and James (1732–94) Adam for the rapidly growing housing developments in Edinburgh, London, Bath and Cheltenham. In some cases wrought and cast iron could be combined to good, and economical, effect, as in the gates of *c.*1767 at Lansdowne House, Berkeley Square, London (fig. 84), built for the Earl of Bute and sold unfinished to William Petty, 1st Marquis of Lansdowne and 2nd Earl of Shelburne, a patron of the arts. Elsewhere in Europe, although change was soon to come, the use of wrought iron continued to flourish.

26. Designs for wrought iron balconies for the Hôtel de Ville, Nancy, France, by Jean Lamour. French, 1752–5. Lamour, blacksmith to King Stanislas of Poland, was one of the masters of the eighteenth century. New York, Cooper-Hewitt Museum, DP 1921-6-210 (5). (Ken Pelka.)

Partie du grand Balcon de L'avant corps du milieu de la Façade de L'hotel de Ville.

Suite du Balcon cy dessus.

Partie du Balcon des angles de la même Façade.

THE NINETEENTH AND TWENTIETH CENTURIES

27. Horse trough; cast iron, Sun Foundry, Glasgow, c. 1880, in Chepstow, Wales. (John Gay.)

28. The Coal Exchange, London; cast iron, 1847–9, designed by J. B. Bunning; demolished 1962. (RCHM.)

In Europe particularly (except perhaps in Spain and Italy) and in North America, the nineteenth century witnessed the flowering of cast iron as the principal material for gates and railings, because it could now be mass produced. Wrought iron was more costly to produce as well as laborious to work. Such was the enthusiasm for cast iron, with its chameleon-like ability to assume the form and appearance of almost all other materials, that it was used for bizarre and sometimes impractical purposes: aquaria, fountains, furniture and water-troughs (fig. 27) and even jewellery. Where cast was substituted directly for wrought iron, it at first took on similar slender forms, so that it is sometimes hard to distinguish between the two. By the 1830s bolder designs appeared, in three-dimensional modelling. Most garden furniture of the time, often decorated with elaborately modelled garden plants, could only have been made in cast iron.

In architecture, cast iron often also masqueraded as something else: stucco in the Doric columns of Carlton House Terrace arcade in Pall Mall, London (1829–33) by John Nash (1752–1835), or carved stone in the Coal Exchange in London (1847–9; fig. 28; now demolished), built by J. B. Bunning (1802–63), of which the V&A has the only surviving three sections. In North America, particularly in iron-rich New York State, the fashion for buildings with fronts made entirely of cast iron (which were regarded as cheap to build and relatively fire proof) led to a boom in the building of department stores (fig. 29), factories and offices. These were designed in a riot of styles – Moorish, Gothic, Renaissance and Classical – and most were built from about 1845 to 1880. Unfortunately these buildings were not as invulnerable to fire as had been expected; cast iron is brittle and shatters if heated and suddenly cooled with water. The largest surviving group of these buildings in the world is today in lower Manhattan, New York City.

29. The Stern Brothers Department Store, West 23rd St, New York City; entirely of cast iron, the largest such façade in the city; 1878–92. Now the New York Merchandise Co. Engraving from *Frank Leslie's Weekly*.

By about 1850, a reaction against the use of cast iron began to be evident in Europe, pioneered by architects who drew their inspiration from the wrought iron of the Middle Ages. Figures such as the historicist architects Viollet-le-Duc (1814–79) in France and Sir George Gilbert Scott (1811–78) in England, did much restoration work on medieval churches and cathedrals, in the course of which they renewed or replaced the wrought iron screens that had earlier been swept away. At the London International Exhibition of 1862 numerous firms showed examples of wrought ironwork in styles that were inspired by the Gothic and the Renaissance (fig. 197). In England the philosophical principles of the architect and designer A. W. N. Pugin (1812–52), the art critic John Ruskin (1819–1900) and the influential craftsman and writer William Morris (1834–96) – all of whom hated modern industrial methods of production, including cast iron – inspired the Arts and Crafts Movement. The revival of artistic craftsmanship that followed, as in the work of the architect of the Law Courts, G.E. Street (1824–81; fig. 111), led to wrought iron being used once again for domestic items like candlesticks, firedogs and fire-irons (fig. 107), with designs that often harked back to the seventeenth and eighteenth centuries.

Between about 1890 and 1914, the emergence of the sinuous organic forms of the Art Nouveau style stimulated much imaginative decorative architectural work in both cast and wrought iron. The most exciting of this was on the Continent: in wrought iron by Victor Horta (1861–1947, who designed his own house in rue Américaine, Brussels (fig. 68) and in cast iron by Hector Guimard (1867–1942) in Paris, the designer most notable for the railings and lamp-standards of the Metro; in wrought iron by designer and craftsman Alessandro Mazzucotelli (1865–1938) in Milan, and in both wrought and cast iron by Antonio Gaudì (1852–1926), the remarkable Art Nouveau architect in Barcelona (fig. 87). In Britain the style's principal exponent was Charles Rennie Mackintosh (1868–1928), the architect notable for the Glasgow School of Art (1896–1909), who designed wrought ironwork of great originality for his buildings in and around Glasgow. Each of these cities still retains some of these masterpieces, but much has been wantonly destroyed.

The First World War marked the beginning of a long period of decline in the architectural and domestic use of all types of ironwork. In the 1920s, however, numerous designs in wrought iron, large and small in scale, were being produced by Edgar Brandt, who designed the gates to the Monument de la Flamme Eternelle in Paris, and Samuel Yellin in Philadelphia. Brandt (1880–1960) produced work characterized by the geometric motifs of Art Deco combined with stylized fruit and flowers (figs 111 right, and 146, right). Yellin (1885–1940), designer of the Episcopalian cathedral of St James in Washington, DC (started 1908), was more eclectic in style, ranging from the neo-Gothic to the neo-Georgian. In the 1920s and 1930s cast iron was also being used all over Europe for the grilles and gates needed for the spate of new buildings then being built.

The Second World War brought to an end this building activity and the attendant demand for ironwork. Had it not, no doubt the Modern Movement in architecture would soon have had the same effect, with its dislike of ornament and preference for unenclosed landscape. Doubtless because of this change in architectural fashion, post-war building activity was accompanied by little interest in the decorative uses of ironwork. Just a few smiths and designers – Raymond Subes of France and Edward Bawden of England, for instance – continued to create iron lighting fixtures and furniture. Only since about 1970 has there been any sign that at least wrought ironwork might find a place in the decoration of a modern building. In this renaissance, Fritz Kühn (1910-67) of East Germany can be seen as a very early pioneer whose gates for the 1958 Brussels World Fair (fig. 90) helped to inspire a generation.

From a 1990s perspective, decorative ironwork falls into three distinct categories: what might be called a 'heritage repro' pastiche, the traditionalist, and the innovative. The last two are largely the preserve of smiths working with mild steel and wrought iron, the first mainly that of foundries producing cast iron. Although much of the work is architectural, a growing proportion is for the domestic interior, especially for lighting and the hearth: candlesticks and brackets, fire-brackets and utensils, chairs and bedsteads.

Items in the 'heritage repro' style now being produced by founders (often in cast aluminium as well as iron) include beds, lamp-posts, gates and garden furniture. Some pieces are direct copies of nineteenth-century patterns (for example, the gates to the White House, Washington, DC; fig. 31), but others are simplifications or exaggerations of basically nineteenth-century patterns, which can result in clumsy and unattractive objects. A sub-class of items, neither cast nor wrought iron, but often misleadingly described as wrought, includes candlesticks, wine-racks, gates and furniture made of iron strip or wire, often crudely sheared off and bent to shape, occasionally adorned with mass-produced, stamped *repoussé* leaves.

Innovative twentieth-century industrial design in cast iron or steel has been almost entirely restricted to domestic wares – cutlery, cooking pots and tea and coffee services – led by the Scandinavians in the 1950s, followed by the British and others in the 1960s, and has been dominated since the 1980s by the Italians, who favour geometric shapes and bright colours. Notable figures are Arne Jacobsen (1902–71) of Denmark architect and designer of stainless steel tableware for Stelton of Copehhagen; and Sigurd Persson (b. 1914) of Sweden, noted for innovative cast iron and stainless steel wares and designer of the new Scandinavian Airlines cutlery service in 1959. Since the 1980s the Italian firm of Alessi of Milan, employing a team of international designers, has been prominent; the stainless steel kettle designed in 1985 by Michael Graves (USA, b. 1934) sold 40,000 in one year alone.

In both Europe and North America, traditionalist smiths tend to produce work inspired by the great age of smithing, the eighteenth century, often for clients whose historic properties combine with their own aesthetically

30. University Museum, Oxford: detail of the roof; glass with cast and wrought iron, stencilled, made by Francis Skidmore of Coventry. English, 1855–60. (Oxford University Museum.)

conservative tastes. Smiths inclined to innovate have made some fine and interesting work for both new developments and old buildings, although designs too purposefully 'original' or using poorly mastered techniques sometimes turn out badly. Much use is made of the power-hammer, a tool that has had great influence on the forms produced, as, unlike hand hammering, it allows substantial masses of iron to be worked at speed. A few powerful blows from the power-hammer will transform solid bars into the beginnings of the spatulate shapes so often found on contemporary work (fig.218).

Today the most remarkable work includes that of Manfred Bergmeister (b. 1927) and Jan Dudesek (b. 1946 figs 127, 138 and 143) of Germany and Switzerland respectively, as well as Albert Paley of Rochester, USA

31. Garden security gates to the White House, Washington DC; cast steel, 1976, after the design of wrought iron gates made by Paul Hedl of New York City, 1818–19, with added eagles and stars, symbols of the American Union. Photograph by Rosamund Solomon. E1575-1991.

(fig. 32), while in Britain the conservatism of the black-smithing tradition has been shrugged off. Striking examples of contemporary British ironwork are the pair of gates in forged stainless steel designed and made by Tony Robinson (b. 1940) for the medieval Great Hall in Winchester Castle (1981–3) and the gates to the V&A Ironwork Gallery by Jim Horrobin (1982).

Buildings as recent as the National Westminster Bank Tower in London (1985) and Lever House in New York City (1952) are bare of decorative ironwork – which would hardly suit their severely functional style of architecture – although the earlier Chrysler Building in New York City (1930) has a distinctive spire of radiant steel arches. It is, however, only just over a century since 1889, when the Eiffel Tower opened, entirely constructed from 9,000 tons of wrought iron. The architectural novelty of its day, it was for years the tallest building in the world, and is a potent reminder of the structural and aesthetic possibilities of the metal. While another such triumph is perhaps unlikely, some of the bold designs recently produced in wrought iron at least suggest that architects and interior designers of the future may use and integrate decorative ironwork in their new buildings, as well as in their restorations of the old.

32. Bench; wrought iron and mahogany, designed by Albert Paley for the V&A Ironwork Gallery, made by Paley Studio. American, 1994. M11-1995.

PART TWO

FORMS AND FUNCTIONS OF DECORATIVE IRONWORK

WINDOWS AND BALCONIES

33. Window grille from the site of the Roman villa at Hinton St Mary, Dorset; wrought iron. Roman, fourth century AD. British Museum, Dept of Prehistoric & Romano-British Antiquities, no. 1966, 2-6, 1. (Trustees of the British Museum.)

From the Middle Ages until the nineteenth century, iron was often used as part of the decoration of windows and balconies. The large glass picture windows in houses today have dimmed our consciousness of the many centuries during which windows were small and open to the elements (the word 'window' is derived from 'wind's eye'). In the sixteenth century glass was introduced into wealthy people's houses, becoming common only in the course of the eighteenth century. Iron grilles, sometimes highly decorative, were therefore used to secure windows from malevolent intruders. Roman houses sometimes had window grilles; star-shaped fragments, and occasionally complete ones, have been found at the sites of houses at Pompeii and Herculaneum in Italy. One of the best preserved is from a fourth-century Romano-British villa

in Dorset (fig. 33). The medieval smith used various decorative motifs: dragons' heads worked into the tops of window-bars, or linked quatrefoils or heart shapes made of iron bar – the last (perhaps as a joke) being on a grille from the House of Jacques Coeur of Dijon (now in Rouen in the Musée Henri le Secq des Tournelles).

After the Renaissance, architects designed far bigger window openings, as demonstrated by the elegant sixteenth-century Italian grilles (fig. 35) or those of *c.*1690 beneath Christopher Wren's library at Trinity College, Cambridge, made by the London smith William Partridge (fig. 37). Contemporary German work is rather more ornate (figs 36 and 39). Window grilles were rarer from the eighteenth century, but in the nineteenth century whole windows, including glazing bars, started to be made in decorative cast iron, often in Gothic shapes. They were probably invented by Thomas Rickman (1776–1841), architect and author of the influential *Glossary of Gothic Architecture*, and made by Thomas Cragg, Rickman's associate from 1812, at his Merseyside foundry.

Iron balconies seem first to appear in Venice in the fourteenth century, but are found in northern European architecture only from the seventeenth century, becoming widespread in the nineteenth century. Some of the great seventeenth-century houses on the Ile St Louis, Paris, are still adorned with their iron balconies, wrought into

34. Balcony front; wrought iron with cast rosettes. French, *c.*1800. 492-1893.

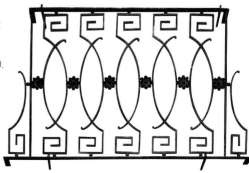

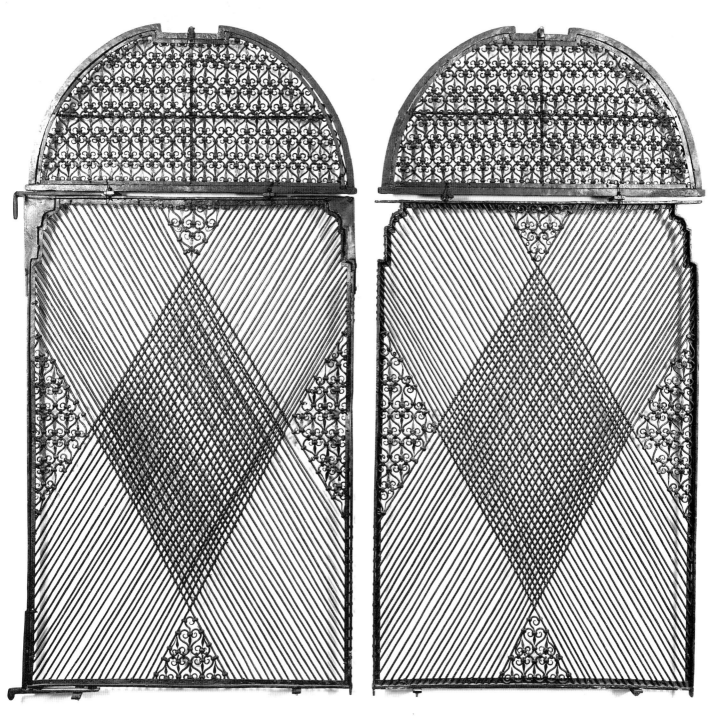

35. Pair of window grilles; wrought iron. Italian, sixteenth century. 125-1879.

restrained Baroque forms, and functioning really as window-guards rather than as true balconies (fig. 34). In the later eighteenth century, English architects such as Robert Adam (1728–92) began to design and install cast iron window-guards – soon termed balconettes – as well as true balconies on the first floor of houses. These were often sheltered beneath iron canopies (fig. 40), originally brightly painted with stripes in imitation of their canvas prototypes. This fashion prevailed in town houses in Britain and North America until about 1840. For the rest of the century, manufacturers, especially in America and Australia, produced ever more elaborate lacy cast iron balconies for first floors, and introduced iron verandahs to ground floors (figs 43–5). This means of extending the living space of a house into the open air was best suited to warm, sunny climates. Today such verandahs and balconies can best be seen on houses in New Orleans, USA (the Pontalba Building of 1848 is an early example), and in Melbourne and Sydney, Australia.

36 (opposite). Window grille from the church of St Nicholas, Aachen; wrought iron. German, seventeenth century. Note the use of round-sectioned bars, typical of German work.
991 & a, 992-1893.

37 (right). Window grilles and screen beneath the Wren Library, Trinity College, Cambridge; wrought iron. Made by William Partridge of London, c.1690. (Author.)

38 (right). Window grille; wrought iron. Italian (?), seventeenth century.
644-1888.

39 (far right). Window grille; wrought iron, with applied work, embossed and engraved. German, seventeenth century. Note the elaborate bars threaded through each other.
5974-1888.

40 (opposite). Balcony with canopy in Edward Square, Islington, London; cast iron, *c.*1830. The design is close to those in L. N. Cottingham, *The Smith's and Founder's Director*, 1824; the canopy would originally have been painted with stripes in imitation of canvas. (John Gay.)

41 (top right). Balcony from No. 1, Impasse des Ecuries, Versailles; wrought iron, with embossed details, originally painted light grey and gilded. French, *c.*1770. The central panel shows the crossed keys and greyhound supporters of the Paris blacksmiths' guild. The monogram, two Ls and two Cs, may represent the initials of Louis XVI and Jean François Cahon, his blacksmith, who bought the house in 1770. M 51-1909.

42 (right). Designs for balcony railings by L. N. Cottingham, 1824.

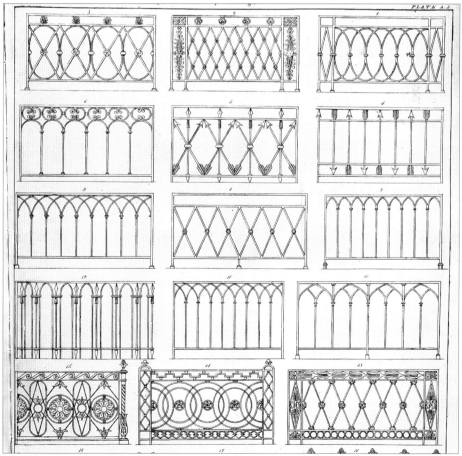

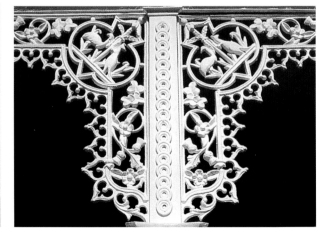

43 (opposite above). Balconies and railings on the 'Villa Residences' (by the architect Thomas Rowe), Darlinghurst, Sydney, NSW; cast iron. Australian, c.1880. Contemporary photograph. E 3128-1995.

44 (opposite below left). Balusters from a verandah; cast iron. Made by H. Sergeant & Co. of Brisbane, Queensland. In commemoration of the foundation of Australia in 1788, this illustration shows aborigines with an emu, a kangaroo and a tree-fern, all unique to Australia. Private collection. (Brian Turner.)

45 (opposite below right). Bracket from a verandah; cast iron. Possibly by H. Sergeant & Co. of Brisbane, Queensland. Australian, 1888. In commemoration of Australia's foundation in 1788, this shows an emu and a kangaroo, together with roses, thistles and shamrocks to symbolise England, Scotland and Ireland. Private collection. (Brian Turner.)

46 (above right). Balconies at the Villino Broggi-Caraceni, Florence; wrought iron. Designed by the architect G. Michelazzi, Italian, c.1911. (Courtauld Institute of Art, Conway Library.)

47 (below right). Window grille at the Maison Rurale, Brussels, Belgium; wrought iron. Designed by the architect De Lastre, c.1905. (Warwick University, History of Art Dept.)

DOORS AND DOOR HARDWARE:
HINGES AND DOOR-KNOCKERS

Outside doors have always needed to be robust to repel unwanted visitors, and iron has long been used for a variety of important door functions – for hinges, handles and door-knockers, although it is rare to find so extensive a pattern of ironwork as that on the fourteenth-century door from Nuremberg in the V&A. Here the wood is almost completely covered with iron sheets embossed all over with the city coat of arms (fig. 49). Leaf and flower shapes were drawn on for hinge designs from the Middle Ages until the nineteenth century.

In the Middle Ages, very elaborate hingework was often made to cover the entire door surface, thus reinforcing as well as decorating it. To judge from surviving examples, mostly on church doors, the English and the Scandinavians were the first to explore the decorative potential of iron on doors, as early as the eleventh century. Numbers of early hinges were shaped as large Cs attached to a strap, the terminals of the Cs being decorated with scrolls or animal heads. This simple form soon developed into patterns of flowing scrolls, as on the St Albans' Abbey hinges (fig. 10) in the V&A. Medieval door handles were simple. As on the Nuremberg door, stout rings of iron were attached to an iron back-plate (often pierced with a pattern in the late Middle Ages) and could serve as both handle and door knocker.

Medieval English and Scandinavian smiths occasionally further embellished doors with abstract iron symbols or, even more rarely, figurative motifs, which probably had a mythical or religious significance, now obscure. Just a few 'picture' doors survive in England, bearing the recurring motifs of a snake, a cross, a dragon, a bird and a ship, but the best examples are found in eastern Sweden, and include scenes of the Crucifixion and the dragon Fafnir. One from Röglösa shows St Michael and the dragon, a bearded devil and hunters and prey (fig. 51).

In the 1240s smiths began stamping iron hingework with stylized leaves and flowers, a technique inspired by contemporary goldsmiths' work. Early examples are on the doors to St George's Chapel, Windsor (fig. 225), and in the Musée de Cluny, Paris, from the doors of Notre Dame Cathedral. A door at Merton College, Oxford (fig. 52), is a rare secular survival of this type, its design showing the close links between secular and ecclesiastical work. Hingework of between 1300 and 1500 often features leaf forms fashioned from sheet iron.

The Renaissance brought a change in the preferred material for door furniture – in parts of Europe, including Italy and France, bronze ousted iron – and hingework was generally concealed. In the north, iron hardware remained popular, smiths from German-speaking lands being especially renowned for their ornate work (figs 49, 50 and 61). Complex hinges were made as much for shutters (fig. 53) and inside doors as for town hall doors (figs 50 and 61). English smiths favoured simpler designs, such as the 'cockspur' type, first evolved c. 1600 (fig. 60). Door handles too became more elaborate.

The mid-eighteenth century front door in Britain and America was remote from the so-called 'Georgian' look favoured today, having just a plain iron door-knob and lock. From around 1800 the fashion grew for decorative cast ironwork, fanlights over the doors and door-knockers (fig. 55). Motifs introduced around 1820 included the sphinx, the dolphin and the lion's head, the latter still popular today and perhaps most famously displayed on the Prime Minister's door at 10 Downing Street.

With rare exceptions, there has been little innovative design of door hardware in the twentieth century; pastiche 'heritage repro' in cast iron is all-prevailing.

48. Door to St Saviour's Church, Dartmouth, Devon; wrought iron on oak. English, c.1390, repaired in 1631, the design inspired by the medieval royal arms of England: three leopards, with stylized leaves typical of the late fourteenth century. (C. Blair.)

49. Door from Nuremberg, Germany; pine covered with embossed sheet iron, with a wrought iron handle. German, c.1400. The coats of arms are, from top left to right, those of: the city of Nuremberg, the single-headed eagle of the German king and the double-tailed lion of the king of Bohemia. This decoration indicates that it was made for a major public building, probably in the reign of Charles IV (r. 1346–78) or of Wenceslas (r. 1376–1400), each of whom was King of both Germany and Bohemia. M 254-1921.

51 (above). Door at Röglösa Church, Östergotland, eastern Sweden; wood with wrought iron mounts. Swedish, c.1200, showing a huntsman and animals at the top, in the centre a devil with flame-like hair and flesh-hook attacking a woman, and on the right a dragon with the winged figure of St Michael, the chief guardian of church sanctuary doors in the Middle Ages here symbolizing the safeguarding of the church. (J. Geddes.)

50. Door to the Town Hall, Sterzing, Tyrol, Austria; wood with wrought iron fittings. Seventeenth century, the floral hinges and elaborate door latch typical of German and Austrian smiths.

52 (right). Hall door at Merton College, Oxford; oak with wrought and stamped iron. English, late thirteenth century. Drawing by W. Denstone, 1868.

53. Shutters; oak with wrought
iron fittings, from a house in
Nuremberg, Germany, c.1550.
Nuremberg was a centre for
all types of metalworking from
the Middle Ages onwards.
2452-1856.

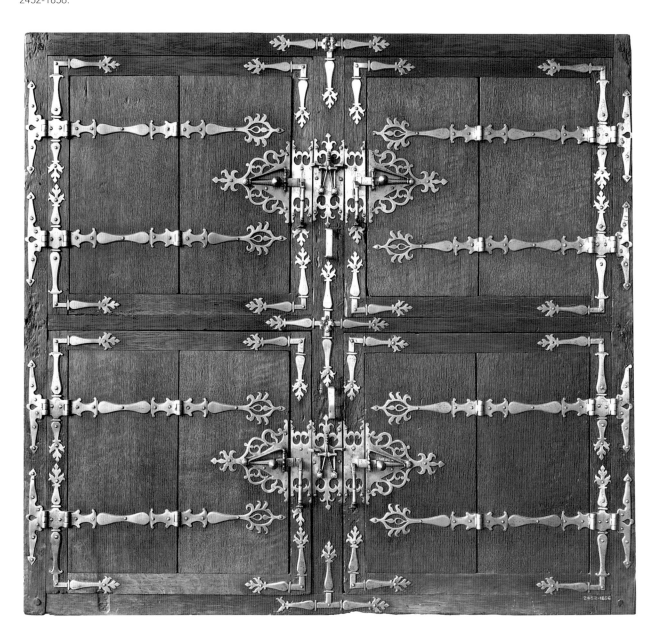

54 (left). Door-knocker; wrought iron. French, nineteenth century. 1219-1855.

55 (below). Door-knockers from London houses; cast iron. English, nineteenth century. Manufacturers often copied each other's patterns. The majority are Neo-classical designs typical of *c*.1820–50; the top right is neo-Renaissance of *c*. 1850–60. M 331-4-1977.

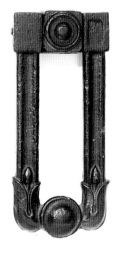

56 (left). Hinge; wrought and stamped iron. French?, fifteenth century. 670-1895.

57 (below). Hinge; wrought and stamped iron. French, thirteenth century, with stamped terminals copied from goldsmiths' work. 473-1895.

58. Door hinge and studs in the University Museum, Oxford; wrought iron by Francis Skidmore of Coventry, 1855–60. As here, Skidmore's designs were much inspired by medieval examples. (Author.)

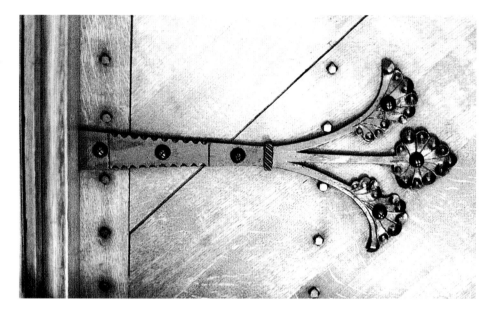

59 (right). Door hinge at King's College, Cambridge; wrought iron. English, sixteenth century; a popular shape with English smiths. (Author.)

60 (below right). Door or cupboard hinge from Suffolk; wrought iron. English, seventeenth century, known from the shape of the ends as a 'cockspur' hinge; typical of English work in the sixteenth and seventeenth centuries. M 236-1922.

61 (far right). Door hinge from Westphalia; wrought and pierced iron, tinned. German seventeenth century. Tinning helped to weatherproof iron. 987-1893.

STAIRCASE BALUSTRADES AND BALUSTERS

Stairs in the Middle Ages were strictly functional, often narrow spirals with simple handrails of rope or wood, if any. The architects of the Renaissance palaces of France and Italy first gave prominence to the grand ceremonial staircase. By about 1550 'open' staircases were being built, requiring substantial balustrades, as in the Palazzo Medici, Florence, with wood or stone upright columns to support the handrail. Iron staircase balustrades seem first to have been made in the seventeenth century, for example in 1688 in the Grand Trianon, Versailles, by Louis Fordrin, and by the eighteenth century they were widespread. Iron combined the qualities of strength and lightness with aesthetic potential, and baluster designs could be as elaborate as the craftsman was skilful or the client wealthy, and could reflect fashionable styles.

One of the earliest iron staircases was designed about 1637 by the architect Inigo Jones (1573–1652) for the Queen's House, Greenwich (fig. 62). Its structure and design, consisting of separately made, repeating motifs of stylized tulips and S shapes, are characteristic of British and American iron staircases right into the twentieth century. In England both S-shaped and lyre-shaped balusters, decorated with acanthus foliage and C scrolls, are typical of the period from about 1700 to 1780. They are sometimes found in the same building, as in Somerset House, London (c. 1775–1801). Here the main 'Royal Academy' staircase is adorned with lyre balusters and another one with simpler S balusters. All were made in the workshop of the London smith William Palmer, to the designs of the architect William Chambers (1723–96), and were painted mid-blue. In the late eighteenth century, the more rigid forms of the Neo-classical revival led to the frequent use of antique motifs in the design of balusters, especially palmettes and honeysuckle (anthemion), as on the cast iron balusters at Osterley House, Middlesex (c.1766), designed by Robert Adam (fig. 65).

By contrast with Britain, continental European balustrade design was both more ambitious and often more sculptural. In France, Italy and Germany, from the seventeenth century onwards, architects made staircases central to their buildings, their wrought iron balustrades often conceived as a continuous whole (figs 63–4 and 66), welded and riveted together as necessary. In the chateau of Compiègne in France, built by King Louis XVI (r.1774–93), the grand 'Escalier du Roi', installed in 1787, was made of wrought iron, partly gilded in two shades of gold, by Raguet, to a Neo-classical design, perhaps by the architect Le Dreux (fig. 67). In Germany, houses were adorned with lush Rococo iron staircases, as in the Rhineland Schloss Brühl, designed around 1743 by Balthasar Neumann (1687–1753).

For much of the nineteenth century, balustrades were manufactured mainly in cast iron, and foundries produced a huge variety of designs. The use of cast iron had a visible effect on design, for it became easy and cheap to make entire sections of elaborate sculptural balustrading, as well as single balusters (fig. 72). In the USA, Louis Sullivan (1856–1924) and Dankmar Adler designed for Chicago some of the most influential buildings in the history of American architecture. Sullivan used ornamented detail prominently in his buildings, with motifs derived from nature (fig. 71). By about 1900 wrought iron was once more in favour, worked into the sinuous forms of Art Nouveau (figs 68–70) to the designs of Louis Majorelle (1859–1926), Victor Horta (1861–1947) and Henri van de Velde (1863–1958). In the late twentieth century, balustrades are rarely of decorative iron, exceptions being work by Albert Paley (for example in the Hyatt Grand Cypress Hotel, Orlando, Florida, 1983) and Takayoshi Komine, who designed the stair rail on the campus of Chukyo University, Japan.

62. The Tulip Staircase; wrought iron, the Queen's House, Greenwich. English, designed by Inigo Jones, c. 1637. (RCHM.)

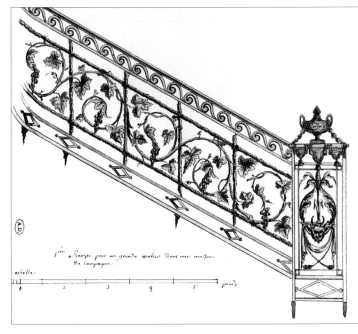

63 (opposite top left). Panel from a staircase, from a house in Augsburg, Germany; wrought iron. German, seventeenth century. 990-1893.

64 (opposite bottom left). Staircase balustrade; wrought iron, embossed and originally painted and gilded. Italian, from Venice, seventeenth century. 5966-1857.

65 (opposite top right). Detail of balusters in Osterley Park House, Middlesex; cast iron and brass. Designed by Robert Adam, British, c.1766.

66 (opposite bottom right). Design for a wrought iron country house staircase. French, c.1800, the vine motif emphasizing the rural setting. Pen and wash, anonymous. Paris, Musée des Arts Décoratifs CD 159. (Musée des Arts Décoratifs; L. Sully-Jaulmes.)

67 (right). The King's Staircase in the royal chateau of Compiègne, Oise, France; cast iron with white and yellow gilding, made by Raguet in 1786 for Louis XVI, possibly after designs by the architect of the house, Le Dreux (1690–1751). The handsome Neo-classical monumentality of the staircase foreshadows the 'Empire' style of the 1800s. (RMN – Arnaudent.)

68 (opposite). Staircase detail in the Musée Horta, Brussels; wrought iron. Belgian, designed by Victor Horta, 1898–1900. Horta, architect and leading exponent of the Art Nouveau style, built the house for his own use. (Courtauld Institute of Art, Conway Library.)

69 (right). Staircase detail in the Karl-Ernst Osthaus Museum, Hagen, Belgium; wrought iron. Belgian, designed by Henri van de Velde, 1901. Van de Velde, architect and architectural historian, built this house for his patron, Osthaus. The style of the skeleton-like stair balusters became a feature of van de Velde's repertoire. (Warwick University, History of Art Department.)

70 (far right). Staircase section; wrought iron, designed and probably made by Louis Majorelle. French, c.1900. Majorelle of Nancy, a major designer of furniture and glass, was also an expert metalworker. Paris, Musée des Arts Décoratifs, inv. 11318. (Musée des Arts Décoratifs.)

71 (right). Staircase section made for the Chicago Stock Exchange, USA (demolished 1972), designed by Louis Sullivan; cast iron, electroplated with copper. American, 1893–4. The oval forms represent seeds, symbols of life, motifs much used by Sullivan in other media. New York, Metropolitan Museum, inv. 1972. 50. 1-4. (Author.)

72 (far right). Balusters from staircases; all are English. Left to right: (a) Wrought iron, with a cast brass rosette plate. Eighteenth century. Private collection. (b) Cast iron, painted olive green. Mid-nineteenth century. M 172-1978.

GATES, FENCES AND RAILINGS

Iron gates and railings, used in the way so familiar today, seem first to have appeared in Europe only in the seventeenth century. Before then, wrought iron gates rarely protected secular buildings, although screens, gates and railings around tombs had been common inside churches since the Middle Ages. At first iron was often used in conjunction with wood for gates and fences, as outside The Durdans, Surrey (fig. 77), the elegant house built shortly before 1689 in a grand 'William and Mary' style by Lord Berkeley. Since the prime function of a fence, however well decorated, was to exclude, the strength and durability of iron ensured that during the eighteenth century iron rather than wood became the chief material for boundary fencing around houses, public buildings and grounds. The gate, the focal point in a fence or wall, allowed the smith to show off his skill, as at Trinity College, Oxford (fig. 79).

The first London square to be enclosed by wrought iron railings was Lincoln's Inn Fields in 1735. Like other early eighteenth-century railings, the design of the uprights was plain, with slightly pointed ends, doubtless a reflection of their simple function as well as of a restricted budget. The commonest other form for the ends of railing uprights, for much of the century, was that of an arrow-head, with flaring barbs. At the opposite end of the aesthetic scale, where show was important and resources substantial, were the gates and screens of the palaces of Versailles, near Paris (1678–9; fig. 81), of Hampton Court, near London (1693; fig. 74–5), and those around the Place Stanislas (formerly Place Royale), Nancy, France (1751–9; fig. 73). All were royal commissions, respectively of Louis XIV of France, William and Mary of England and King Stanislas of Poland, given to outstanding smiths who deployed their every skill.

73. Fountain Screen, Place Stanislas, Nancy; wrought iron, embossed and gilt, by Jean Lamour. French, 1751–9.

Luchet's restrained Classicism at Versailles and the novel and the lavish use of embossed ornament at Hampton Court by Jean Tijou (fl. 1689–1712) were as notable as the powerful Rococo idiom at Nancy of Jean Lamour (1698–1771); all incorporated apt heraldic motifs into their work, a feature much found later too.

From about 1790 and for the majority of the nineteenth century, cast iron ousted wrought for gates and railings in much of Europe and North America. Just a few cast iron railings had been produced earlier; amongst the first were those made for the Senate House, Cambridge. This design was not emulated in the nineteenth century; founders preferred slim uprights with a variety of finials: spears, javelins, leaves, flowers, especially the honeysuckle (figs 84–6), and acorns. From about 1850 gates and railings became increasingly heavy and ornate (fig. 76). Partly in reaction to this, and as a result of the influence of William Morris and his circle, from about 1880 wrought iron became fashionable once more (fig. 86).

For much of the twentieth century, decorative railings and gates were less often made, partly because older work remained *in situ* but also because the Modern Movement architects of new buildings had political as well as aesthetic objections to them. Huge damage was done throughout Europe in the Second World War, both by bombing and by the systematic removal of railings for recycling into munitions. Ultimately, however, from the 1970s, this destruction created a need for, and helped regenerate interest in, decorative iron fencing for modern buildings. Fritz Kühn (1910–67) of Germany was a pioneer in this revival; and the restrained symmetry of his 1958 Brussels gates led later to the audacity of Paley's Chattanooga fence of 1975 (fig. 89) and the elegance of recently made gates at Oxford (fig. 90), at St Hugh's College, in 1988, designed by Lawrence Whistler (b. 1912), and at St John's College, designed in 1993 by the jeweller Wendy Ramshaw (b. 1940; fig. 88).

74 (below). Design for the Fountain Garden screen, Hampton Court, near London. English, by Jean Tijou, 1693. The design and the gates as built are slightly different. Tijou drew inspiration from the work of earlier French designers, Jean de Mortin of c.1640 and Hugues Brisville of 1663, and some of his designs derive from the iron-work of c.1680 at Versailles. Engraving from Tijou's *The New Booke of Drawings*.

75 (bottom left). Satyr mask from the Fountain Garden screen, Hampton Court; wrought iron, embossed. English by Jean Tijou, c.1893. Lent by Historic Royal Palaces.

76 (bottom right). Detail of fence around the Dakota Apartments, New York City, USA; cast iron by the Hecla Ironworks of Brooklyn, New York City, 1884. The Dakota, by the architect Henry Hardenbergh, was the city's first luxury apartment building in German Renaissance style. (Author.)

77. View of Lord Berkeley's New House, The Durdans, Surrey; oil on canvas, signed by Jacob Scmits (d.1694), dated 1689. Plain dark iron fencing flanks the doorway above which is an iron balcony, apparently painted white with gilding. The gate and fence in the foreground combine a wooden framework with slender iron rails, a combination generally replaced by iron in the eighteenth century. All are painted light grey which, with white, was fashionable for ironwork at this date. Private collection. (Trustees of the Berkeley Will Trust.)

79. Gate in Trinity College, Oxford, in wrought iron. English,1713, probably by Thomas Robinson of London. The symmetrical design is typically English. The lines of arrow-heads at ground level are anti-dog devices or 'dog bars'. Ink and wash drawing by A. E. Gerrard, 1938. Oxford, Bodleian Library, MS Top. Oxon. a. 70. (Bodleian Library.)

78 (top left). Garden gates; wrought iron, Upper Belvedere, Vienna, Austria. Possibly designed, like the Palace, by Lukas von Hildebrandt.1721-3. (A. F. Kersting.)

80 (above). The White Gates at Leeswood Hall, Clwyd, North Wales; wrought and embossed iron painted white, made in 1726 by Robert Davies (d.1748) for Sir George Wynne, perhaps to the design of the architect Henry Flitcroft (1697–1769). This remarkable ensemble in the Palladian style was intended to be seen in a garden landscape. (A.F. Kersting.)

81 (left). Detail of the gate and railing around the chateau of Versailles, France, of wrought iron, made by Luchet 1678–9 for Louis XIV. These lance-headed railings are early examples of a design that became commonplace in the late eighteenth century. Decorative motifs, such as interlaced Ls, fleurs-de-lis and crowns, allude to the royal nature of the commission. Ink and wash drawing by J. Lechevin, dated 1694. Paris, Musée des Arts Décoratifs, no. 8503. (Musée des Arts Décoratifs – L. Sully-Jaulmes.)

82 (below). Cresting for a gateway from East Dean Manor House, Hants; wrought iron. English, eighteenth century. The cypher, perhaps 'CAW', alluded to the unknown commissioner of the work. M 353-1926.

83. Gates; wrought iron, embossed. German, c.1740, originally painted dark blue with gilding. M 5 & a-1981.

84. Garden gates from Lansdowne House, Berkeley Square, London (removed 1930s); cast iron and wrought iron. Designed c.1767 by Robert Adam; the house was sold unfinished to a great patron of the arts, the 1st Marquis of Lansdowne. The stylized heart and honeysuckle motifs were much used by Adam. The cast beehives on the gate-piers allude to the family crest of the Lansdownes. M 1-1961.

85 (right). Railing finials in Edinburgh; cast iron. Scottish, c.1820-40. (John Gay.)

86 (far right). Gates to the Law Courts, London; wrought iron, designed by the architect of the building, G. E. Street, 1866–82, made by Potter of London, decorated with the repeated monogram 'VR' for Queen Victoria. (Courtauld Institute of Art, Conway Library.)

87. Dragon Gate entrance to the Güell House, Barcelona, Spain; wrought iron, designed by the architect Antoni Gaudì (1852–1926), and possibly made by Josep-Maria Jujol.

Spanish, 1884–7. Gaudì was the son of a coppersmith, and used metalwork with great sympathy to enhance the visual effect of his architecture. (Tim Benton.)

88. Garden gate at St John's College, Oxford; wrought iron and magnifying glass, designed by Wendy Ramshaw. English, 1993. (Author.)

89. Fence around the Hunter Museum of Art, Chattanooga, Tennessee, USA; wrought mild steel, made by Albert Paley, 1975. (A. Paley.)

90 (above). The Swan Gates at St Hugh's College, Oxford; wrought iron, 1986. Designed by Laurence Whistler (b. 1912), made by R. Quinnell.

91 (right). Grille by Klaus Waltz; wrought iron, c.1980. M 947-1983.

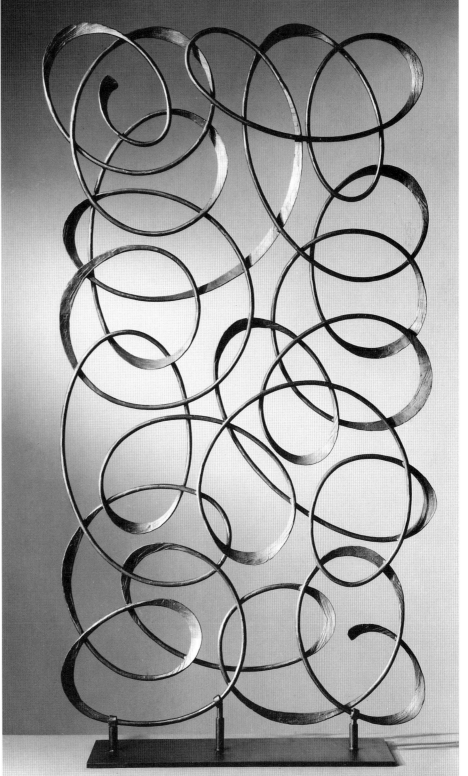

TRADE-SIGNS AND INN-SIGNS

92. London shop-signs, Cornhill, looking towards St Paul's Cathedral; engraving, c.1750, by Thomas Bowles.

Until the nineteenth century, trade-signs, often made of iron, enlivened many European streets. They acted as indicators of the sort of trade being carried out, or the goods being marketed within the premises. Signs also allowed private houses and institutions to be readily identified in a large town or city – particularly necessary before the nineteenth-century introduction of house numbering and street signs and in an age when illiteracy was still widespread.

Trade-signs, precursors of both the modern neon sign and the logo, were designed to be at once eye catching and memorable. Although some Roman signs, as at Ostia in Italy, were of mosaic, those in early modern times were generally of carved wood or stone. By the seventeenth century, however, in London and Paris they were being made of wrought or sometimes sheet iron, which was durable, decorative and could be brightly painted. The bracket supporting the sign, often also elaborately wrought, was usually attached to the house wall, but was sometimes freestanding. The motif chosen for the sign would be appropriate and recognizable, often being taken from the crest or coat of arms of a family or craft guild (figs 93–4), such as keys for a locksmith (fig. 95), or horseshoes and donkey-shoes for a farrier (fig. 96), or a helm for an armourer (fig. 97). Sometimes the image of a saint would evoke the trade, for example the Parisian pork butcher whose shop-sign showed St Anthony of Padua with his pig (fig. 98). Inn and tavern signs were aptly embellished with vine-leaves and grapes, or barley and hops, unless they embodied the name of the inn. Ingenious word play was sometimes involved, as in the case of the tavern called 'L'Age d'Or' or 'L'H d'Or' ('The Golden Age' or 'The Golden H'), whose sign was a golden axe, the French for which, *l'hache d'or*, sounds almost the same (fig. 93).

The very success of trade-signs as decoration led to their demise. As blacksmiths grew more competitive and their designs bolder, so the signs grew larger and heavier. Accidents included four people being killed in the City of London in 1718, the collapse of house fronts under the weight of the signs and injury to passers-by hit by falling parts. In the 1660s the London and Paris authorities attempted to control the situation. In London it was forbidden to hang signs right across the streets and it was ordered that they should be fixed to balconies or houses; a Parisian regulation of 1669 laid down the maximum permissible dimensions and projection of all such signs. A century later, further legislation indicates that these

93. Inn-sign 'A L'H D'OR'
(meaning 'The Golden Axe');
wrought iron, the axe formerly
gilt. French, eighteenth
century. The unknown original
proprietor has incorporated
his initials, 'DM'; probably
from Paris. Rouen, Musée le
Secq des Tournelles, LS 4532.
(Rouen Museums.)

rules had been ignored. In 1761 in Paris all projecting signs were banned and wall-mounted plaques were stipulated instead, and from about this date London parishes began ordering the removal of all projecting signs. However, numbers survived in place in both cities until the building boom of the second half of the nineteenth century, when most were destroyed with their supporting buildings. Some French signs were saved, collected most notably by Henri le Secq des Tournelles, and can today be seen in his museum in Rouen; others are preserved in the Musée Carnavalet, Paris. No such collection exists in England. Elsewhere in Europe, however, especially in Austria (Salzburg) and Germany (Augsburg) and in Switzerland, smiths continued to make signs, and still do.

94 (opposite, top left). Plaque with arms of the Salters' Company of London; cast iron, English, c.1820, originally set into the wall. The motto 'salt savours all' accompanies salt cellars of nineteenth-century shape. M 377-1912.

95 (opposite, top right). Inn-sign; sheet iron, cut, gilded and painted. English, c.1951. The panel, in the shape of a swan, is thought to have been made for the 1951 Festival of Britain, held on the South Bank, London. L 2545.

96 (opposite, bottom left). Farrier's sign; wrought iron. French, eighteenth century, showing the tools of the trade and 'St Eloi's bouquet', the cluster of horseshoes used for horses, mules and cattle. Rouen, Musée le Secq des Tournelles, inv. LS 4039. (Rouen Museums.)

97 (opposite, bottom right). Armourer's sign in the shape of a plumed helm; wrought and sheet iron. French, c.1800, from an unknown Paris shop. Paris, Musée Carnavalet, EN 030. (Spadem.)

98 (above right). Plaque of St Anthony with his pigs; cast iron. French, c.1800, from an unknown Paris pork butcher's shop, where it was set into the wall. Paris, Musée Carnavalet, EN 59. (Spadem.)

99 (right). Locksmith's sign; wrought iron. German, late eighteenth century. 545-1869.

WEATHER-VANES

Wind indicators or weather-vanes in the form of elaborate mobile images made of metal, placed high on buildings, have a long history. Wind direction has always been a good indicator of the weather to come, a vital consideration to all societies with economies dependent on agriculture or fishing. An early recorded example was the mobile bronze Triton which surmounted the Tower of the Winds in Athens in 100 BC. Weather-vanes could take many shapes. The word 'vane' derives from *fahne*, the Anglo-Saxon and Old German for 'flag' and indicates that an early type was flag shaped, probably pierced or painted with symbols of ownership, such as initials, a coat of arms or a heraldic badge, often an animal like a lion or dragon (fig. 102). Few pre-eighteenth-century weather-vanes survive in place, one such being on the tower of Oxburgh Hall in Norfolk, where the sheet iron vane is pierced with the elaborate ancestral arms of the owners, the Paston and Bedingfield families, as used in about 1660.

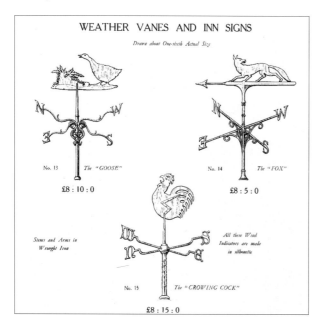

Weather-cocks were apparently a popular form in England even before the Conquest, when manuscripts depict them atop such important buildings as churches and palaces. Their supports sometimes show distinctive scrollwork, which suggests that they were made at least in part of wrought iron. Weather-cocks have remained one of the most popular designs, although it is almost impossible to date the majority without other evidence. The constituent parts of a 1933 design for weather-cocks (fig. 100) seem to have evolved at different dates; by the mid-seventeenth century the arrow-shaped pointer had been added to the mobile image, and the cardinal points of the compass appear by about 1700.

Designs used over the centuries have included the figures of saints and angels, men and women, animals, birds, fish and boats, in wrought or sheet iron. The cathedral of St Bavo in Ghent, Belgium, was once surmounted by a dragon weather-vane, and the sixteenth-century Royal Exchange building in London was topped by a weather-vane of a grasshopper, which was the family badge of its builder, the financier Sir Thomas Gresham.

Weather-vanes continue to offer great possibilities for sculptural expression, and today more abstract forms are being produced in wrought iron, as well as figurative work, often in sheet iron (fig. 101).

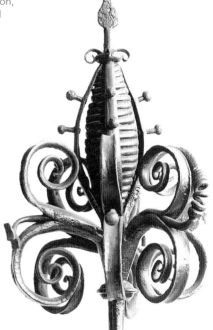

103. Weather-vane from Woodcote House, Carshalton, Surrey; wrought iron, dated 1758. English. M 70-1955.

100 (opposite, below). Catalogue patterns for wrought iron weather-vanes, by Thomas Elsley, London, 1933.

101 (opposite, above). Weather-vane; wrought and welded steel, by Brent Kington, Illinois, USA, 1979. Private collection.

102 (right). Weather-vane from a church; wrought iron. German, seventeenth century. 9040-1863.

FIREDOGS AND FIREBACKS

Until relatively recently, for many families the fireplace was the focus of the house and the prime source of heat. Wood was the main fuel until the seventeenth century, and to burn it efficiently firedogs (also called andirons or cobirons) and, later, firebacks were used. The development of both is related to that of the hearth itself. The earliest domestic fires were in the middle of the room, and the smoke had to escape through a hole (louvre) in the roof. Fireplaces set against the wall, with chimneys for drawing the smoke, were known in Europe from the eleventh century, but were found only in the grandest houses and castles until about 1500, after which they became more widespread (fig. 104). Iron firebacks and firedogs encouraged efficient fuel use.

It is not known at what date firedogs were first used. Their function is to lift the logs off the floor and allow a draught under the fire to help it burn. Celtic firedogs have been found in various parts of Europe, often wrought with horses' heads (fig. 8). In the Middle Ages their form was simpler; uprights might be curved into a swan's neck or might support a cup-shaped bracket, useful for holding a flask of warm ale. They were used sometimes singly (fig. 105), sometimes in pairs. In the sixteenth century the production of cast-iron firedogs began on a large scale, and the making of wrought iron dogs probably diminished, both being superseded by the firegrates of the eighteenth century.

Firebacks protected the hearth's chimney wall from the fire, and threw some of the heat back into the room. Always made of cast iron, their decorative potential was at once realized by the iron founders. Designs were created by pressing wooden or other stamps, or a single wood pattern or model, into a mass of wet sand on the foundry floor. The molten iron was then poured into the resulting depression and cooled. Early English examples are simple, often with a single motif repeated. Sometimes real objects were used to make up patterns, such as daggers, rope or even butter-moulds, and inscriptions were made up of separate letters, sometimes wrongly assembled by an unlettered founder.

Wooden patterns carved with a whole fireback design were introduced in about 1550. In the seventeenth century heraldic coats of arms became popular everywhere, as were pictorial scenes, particularly with biblical or political significance (fig. 112). The seventeenth-century Dutch favoured flower motifs for their firebacks (doubtless related to their interest in painting flowers and this fashion was followed by the English, probably influenced by the accession to the British throne of the Dutch William III (r. 1689–1702). Although the need for firebacks and firedogs dwindled in the eighteenth century with the development of coal-burning grates, and the growing sophistication of wood-burning stoves, both backs and dogs continued to be made. The revival of the use of open fireplaces in the twentieth century has led to the replica casting of many old patterns, as well as to a few new designs (fig. 111).

104. Fireback and firedogs at Ockwell Manor, Berks; cast iron. English, dated 1565; the initials 'ER' may be those either of the owner or of the then monarch, Elizabeth I. Private collection.

105. Virgin and Child, set in an interior; oil on oak, workshop of Robert Campin, c.1435. A single firedog (common at this date) appears to support a modest fire. A shovel under the logs adds support. London, National Gallery, NG 6514. (National Gallery.)

106. The Lenard fireback; cast iron. English (Sussex), dated 1636, inscribed 'Richard Lenard founder at Bred fournis'. Lenard inherited the Brede Foundry in Sussex in 1605, and is here surrounded by the tools and products of his trade – a rare contemporary record of the industry. Several versions of this exist. Lewes, Anne of Cleves House Museum. (Lewes Museum.)

108 (below). Firedog; French, seventeenth century, from Dijon; the hooks at the front were to hold spits, the bracket at the top to hold a flask. M 656-1905.

107 (below). Firedogs in cast iron (although shown here singly, they were used in pairs). (left) German, late fifteenth century, from Rott, near Cornelymünster. 1016-1893. (right) English, seventeenth century, with the initials 'WI'. 899-1901.

109 (above). Designs for firedogs in cast iron by Barbezat & Cie. of Paris, 1858, include famous figures in French history such as Napoleon and Josephine. Engraving in catalogue.

110. Fireback; cast iron. American, dated 1767, inscribed 'A. T. New York'. The costume of the man, with plumed hat and sword, and the style of the fireback, are typically seventeenth-century Dutch and suggest that the founder has adapted an old pattern. New York, called New Amsterdam until 1664, had strong Dutch links. New York, Metropolitan Museum of Art, 16.145 or 44.126. (Metropolitan Museum.)

112 (below). Fireback; cast iron. Dutch, c.1650, with the figure of Hollandia and the lion of the United Provinces. Pomegranates, symbols for the unity of many under one authority, frequently appear on the borders of Dutch firebacks alluding to the struggles for unification of the Provinces. M 1411-1926.

111. Firedogs in wrought iron: (left) English, designed by C.R. Ashbee and made by the Guild of Handicraft, 1900–5, with a copper and brass rosette as finial. Circ 295-1959. (right) French, stamped 'MADE IN FRANCE. E. BRANDT', c.1930; the grape-motif finial partly embellished with bronze. M 88-1979.

HEATING: FIREGRATES AND STOVES

The open hearth, where wood was burned against a fireback and rested on firedogs, was fuel hungry and hugely inefficient – around 90% of the heat went up the chimney. The development of both the firegrate and the stove was directly linked to these problems. By the late sixteenth century a growing shortage of wood, particularly in Britain, led to the domestic use of a new fuel, sea-coal. As coal fires needed more air than wood to keep them alight, they did not burn well resting on an open hearth and it became necessary to redesign fire equipment. A simple means of encouraging combustion was devised: the firegrate, a framework of iron bars raised off the ground on feet (fig. 113).

Even so, open coal-burning fires were inefficient and barely adequate for the relatively mild French and British winters. The Italians and Spanish tended to use portable charcoal burning braziers, occasionally supplemented by wood fires. The design of early grates often included residual features from the past, such as fireback-like back panels, while firedogs were sometimes adapted to support the firebasket. By about 1750 firegrates could be entirely freestanding (figs 116 and 117). Some of the most elegant were designed by the British architect Robert Adam and made by the Carron Company of Scotland (fig. 123). Fire-irons became less robust and more purely decorative, and coal fires needed

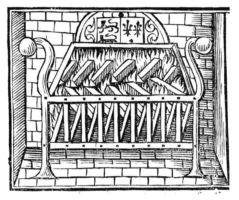

113 (above). Firegrate; wrought iron with cast back panel showing the English royal arms. Printed in 1644, at a time of continuing severe fuel shortage in England, this shows a grate for burning 'artificial coale for rich and poore', bricks made of clay, straw and sea-coal, probably typical of contemporary coal-burning grates. Woodcut from Robert Lemon, *Catalogue of Printed Broadsides*, 1866. (Society of Antiquaries of London.)

new tools like the poker (fig. 126), which was used to separate and to aerate the coal.

A more efficient alternative, especially in America, was the stove-grate, essentially an open-fronted stove designed to fit into a fireplace aperture, with a centrally placed door which could be shut to maximize the heat or opened to allow the fire to be seen. The most famous design was that perfected in 1742 by the statesman and inventor Benjamin Franklin (1706–90) and cast by Robert Grace of Philadelphia, Penn. Such stoves were widely made and were called either a Pennsylvania fireplace or a Franklin stove (fig. 116).

From about 1770 hob grates (fig. 121) were made, often for smaller hearths than hitherto. These grates were set into the fireplace with a hob on either side of the basket to rest a kettle. Numerous further modifications were invented over the next century in order to increase the heat emitted by the grate and to prevent it smoking. An important one was the register grate (fig. 117), which included an iron plate (the register) to adjust the size of the chimney opening and enable the smoke to escape without taking all the warm air with it. The 'apostle of fireside comfort', Benjamin Thompson (1753-1814) of New Hampshire, USA, pioneered other improvements, like lowering the firebasket, reducing the aperture, adding a hood and lining the grate with firebrick. Whilst heating was improved inside, the resultant atmospheric pollution outside led to worsening toxic fogs. In the course of the twentieth century many cities have banned coal and wood-burning fires, so that grate production has declined dramatically.

An efficient heating system was essential to survive the intense winter cold of northern Europe and of the north-

114. Living room interior with tier-stove of cast iron, decorated with scrollwork. The poles around it were for drying and airing washing. German, 1736, ink and wash drawing, Nuremberg, Germanisches Nationalmuseum. (Germanisches Nationalmuseum.)

ern USA and Canada, and this stimulated the development of the iron stove in many shapes. Ceramic and brick stoves first appear in medieval Germany and Austria, possibly derived from Chinese prototypes. Iron stoves were probably developed in fifteenth-century Germany; they could be smaller than brick ones and gave off heat faster. They were basically freestanding, box-shaped structures which contained the burning fuel. They were made up of rectangular cast stove plates, bolted together, which were made in the same way as firebacks, but were usually thinner and lighter, decorated with heraldic and religious motifs (figs 114, 119 and 120). Just such a stove is in the Grosse Hofstube in the castle at at West Coburg, Germany, dated 1501, and is the only intact Gothic stove known.

At first these stoves seem to have been luxury objects, the models for their plates having designs inspired by contemporary woodcuts and engravings. By the late sixteenth century production had increased, and combination iron and ceramic stoves were made (fig. 119) to harness the best properties of each material, iron being quick to heat and ceramic good at radiating stored heat as the fire cooled. These combination stoves were made in German and Scandinavian countries until the nineteenth century. Eighteenth-century improvements in iron casting allowed the production of new shapes: the cylinder, the pyramid and the urn (figs 117 and 123), and

technological improvements harnessed hot air and smoke for extra heat. Stoves became fashionable in France and Britain too; manufacturers included Abraham Buzaglo (1716–88) of London, who offered eleven different styles of his stove, patented in 1765, to burn peat, coal or wood, and who exported at least one to America (fig. 120).

In the nineteenth century, however, it was America's turn to dominate the market. From 1820 to 1890 the Hudson River towns of Albany and Troy in New York State – close to good transport and fine raw materials – were outstanding producers and exporters of stoves – many being box stoves or six-plate stoves, portable and inexpensive. An observer in the 1840s states: 'llamas have carried Troy stoves across the Andes ... camels to the shores of the Black Sea, and ships to Turkey, China, Japan, Australia'. In one year, 1875, the two towns manufactured 450,000 stoves, which then retailed at between $4 and $40.

Stove technology paved the way for the invention of modern central heating systems which by the mid-twentieth century had made all but a few manufacturers redundant. Since the 1970s ecological concerns, fuel crises and the heritage factor in Europe and America have combined to create an interest in using and restoring old grates (often to hold gas-powered 'burning' coals) and stoves, as well as in commissioning new firegrates and irons (fig. 127).

115 (opposite). Tula fireplace; steel, burnished with applied decoration of gilt copper, brass and cut steel. Russian, made at the Imperial Arms Factory at Tula near Moscow, late eighteenth century. The principal Russian arms factory at Tula, established in 1705, began to produce luxury furniture made of steel, blued or burnished, and embellished with copper and brass, from c.1760. The ornaments of the mantlepiece here include in the centre a perfume-burner. Catherine Wilmot wrote home from Russia in 1806: 'the Curiosity from Tula is a machine for perfuming rooms. Its office I suppose will now be to lie quietly on the steel chimney piece.' M 49-1953.

116 (above right). Franklin stove-grate; cast iron, made by Jones & Weed of Philadelphia, USA. American, 1805–8. Designed to be wood-burning and placed in a traditional hearth with a flue going up the chimney. The doors could be shut over the flames to increase heat, or left open for show, and the heating pipes circulated the hot air. The design was the invention in 1742 of Benjamin Franklin, famous statesman and scientist. Winterthur Museum no. 83.0210. (Winterthur Museum.)

117 (right). Trade card of Henry Jackson, London. English, c.1777. The advertising leaflet of its day, this shows the variety of fireplaces and stoves available. Register stoves can be seen on the lower left and right. Engraving. British Museum, Dept of Prints and Drawings, Banks Collection, no. D 2107. (Trustees of the British Museum.)

118. Stove-plate; cast iron. German or Flemish, c.1500, showing St James of Compostella dressed as a pilgrim with cockle-shell hat-badge, and St Peter with key. Several wooden patterns have been used to make up the design, their edges clearly visible. The notches along the edges show where the fixing rods held the plate in place. M 334-1940.

119 (left). Tier-stove; cast iron and ceramic. German, c.1600, in the castle chapel at Wilhelmsburg, Schmalkalden, Germany. The lowest part is made up of five separately cast plates, held together with fixing rods, decorated with biblical scenes including (front) the marriage feast of Cana. The top two tiers are glazed ceramic.

120. Tier-stove; cast iron, made by Abraham Buzaglo, dated 1770, for the then governor of Virginia, Lord Boretourt. The only other complete Buzaglo stove is at Knole House, Kent. Buzaglo was an authority on gout, which was alleviated by warmth. The Colonial Williamsburg Foundation, Virginia, USA, L 1933–503. (Colonial Williamsburg Foundation.)

121. Firegrate; wrought iron, designed by the designer Eugène Grasset (1845-1917). French, c.1890. Paris, Musée des Arts Décoratifs, no. 45714. (Musée des Arts Décoratifs – L. Sully-Jaulmes.)

122. Wrought mild steel firegrate, with bronze. English, by Antony Robinson, 1979. Robinson's work includes the spectacular gates in the medieval Great Hall at Winchester Castle, made 1981–3. M75-1979.

123 (above). Stove from Compton Place, Eastbourne; cast iron. British, late eighteenth century. Probably designed by Robert Adam and made by the Carron Company in Falkirk, Scotland, where a similar stove heated the general offices. Others designed by Adam are at Kedleston Hall, Derbys. M 3-1920.

124. Stove design in cast iron, c.1850–80, by the Havstad Foundry, Arendal, Norway, decorated with rustic figures amidst neo-Rococo scrollwork.

126 (left). Engraving of fire-irons in steel, cast and polished, made by Turner of Sheffield, c.1850.

127 (below). Fire-irons; wrought mild steel by Jan Dudesek. Swiss, c.1980. Private collection.

125. Parlour stove; cast iron by Low & Leake, Albany, New York, USA, dated 1844. Decorated patriotically with the American eagle; the S-scroll supports are flues to allow the hot air to circulate. Albany Institute Collection, USA. (Albany Institute.)

DOMESTIC INTERIORS: THE HEARTH

THE COOKING HEARTH AND ITS EQUIPMENT

Only the wealthy had separate kitchens in the Middle Ages. In many countries and societies, for many centuries, one fireplace served all the needs of the household.

Through the Middle Ages and into the eighteenth century, stewing and grilling were the principal means of cooking for most people. Pots and cauldrons, of iron or bronze, were suspended over the fire (figs 133 and 137), either on iron pot-hooks designed to hold them at different heights or on more elaborate chimney-cranes, which were set into the wall beside the fire and could be swung into position when needed. Iron trivets (three or four-footed stands) or grid-irons (figs 131 and 136), placed beside the fire, supported and kept warm kettles, cooking-pots and plates. Iron griddles were used for baking bread, scones and oat-cakes over the fire. In the seventeenth and eighteenth centuries, in such countries as Germany and Belgium, holy wafers, as well as waffles for domestic consumption, were made by pouring batter into heated wafering-irons, which were often engraved with elaborate patterns (fig. 130). Iron toasting-forks, generally freestanding (fig. 139), were used not just for bread, but also to grill fish, small game birds and cuts of meat. Alternatively, these could be cooked on an iron spit, which was supported at each end by specially made hooks on the fronts of firedogs (figs 108 and 128).

For centuries, joints of roast meat, and large birds like swans and peacocks, were affordable only to a minority. Cooking was slow, on large iron spits, which in the Middle Ages were often turned by boys (fig.128). By the seventeenth century iron spit-jacks were becoming more usual; their simple cranking mechanism enabled the spit to rotate steadily. Notoriously these were sometimes powered by small well-trained dogs, running on the spot inside a wheel linked to the spit (fig. 129).

In the eighteenth century, the cooking hearth began to be revolutionized by the introduction of the coal-burning open range. This had a fire-basket, with horizontal panels on either side, on which pots could rest; a further improvement was a side oven (fig. 131).

It was not until the appearance of the closed range in the nineteenth century that the equipment of the open hearth finally became obsolete. Closed ranges – made of cast iron, sparingly decorated – were essentially the ancestors of the modern cooker (fig. 132). They were more fuel efficient, easier to control and more hygienic since pots no longer came into direct contact with the fire. Although coal-burning ranges were widely replaced in the 1930s by gas and electric cookers, modern equivalents like the Aga (made of enamelled cast iron) are still in use today.

128 (opposite). Manuscript illustration of spit-roasting, the iron spit supported on a firedog, with iron dripping-pan and ladle. Dutch, *c.*1440; detail of an illuminated leaf from the Hours of Catherine of Cleves. New York, Pierpont Morgan Library, M. 917, f.101. (New York, Trustees of the Pierpont Morgan Library.)

129 (above). Kitchen interior at an inn in Newcastle, South Wales, *c.*1797, showing an open iron range, with the spit being turned by a dog, iron basting spoon and tray beneath the joint; aquatint after Thomas Rowlandson, from H. Wigstead, *Remarks on a Tour to North and South Wales in 1797.*

130 (right). Waffle-making with a wafering-iron; oil painting by Pieter Aerstzen. Dutch, *c.*1550. Private collection.

131. Design for an open range in cast iron, by Skidmore of London, 1811, showing two trivets attached to the stove bars for pans to be heated over the flames, and three ovens to the right. Engraving in contemporary catalogue.

132. The Hattersley closed range; cast iron, patented 1890. The flues for the two ovens were frequently arranged to provide bottom heat for one oven for baking and top heat for the other oven, to make it more suitable for roasting. Private collection.

134 (above). Rack of cooking implements; wrought steel and cast brass. Flemish or Dutch, c.1700. From left to right: a skimmer, two ladles, a soot-rake, tongs and shovel for use in the kitchen. M 121-g-1925.

133. Pot-hanger and pot. French, eighteenth century. The pot-hanger of wrought iron has a ratchet at the top to allow its height to be adjusted over the flames. The stew pot of cast iron is decorated with a hunting scene and inscribed 'PIERRE ROSE' and 'MARIE'. It was a wedding present, its shape distinctively French. Rouen, Musée le Secq des Tournelles, no. 3530. (Author.)

135. Kettle; cast iron. American, nineteenth century. A robust casting, the shape a forerunner of the modern mass-produced steel kettle. Albany Institute of Art, New York State. (Albany Institute.)

136. Trivet; wrought iron.
English or Flemish, eighteenth
century. 581-1905.

137. Pot-hook; wrought iron.
English, eighteenth century.
With an open hearth the only
means of controlling heat was
by adjusting the height of
cooking pots suspended on
pot-hooks over the fire. The
introduction of the enclosed
range in the eighteenth
century made pot-hooks
redundant. The ratcheted
teeth and loosely hinged hasp
allowed the pot-hook to be
lengthened or shortened. This
example is unusually
ornamental, pierced with a
design of a blacksmith at his
anvil with the tools of his
trade. 496-1902.

138 (above). Griddle by Jan Dudesek; wrought iron. Swiss, c.1980.

139. Toasters:
(below left). Trivet with toasting fork; wrought iron. English, eighteenth century.

This multi-purpose piece was intended for use in front of a grate or raised hearth. The design allowed several slices of bread or chops or small birds to be roasted at once. The height of the forks could be adjusted as required, and the stand or trivet is tall enough to be used

independently to warm plates or bowls of food over the fire. 790&-a-1902.

(right). Standing toaster; wrought iron. English, eighteenth century. For use in front of a raised hearth or grate. Prongs fitted into the sliding back to secure the cooking meat, and the ring underneath would have supported a dish to catch the dripping juices. 4-1893.

LIGHTING INSIDE

From remote antiquity until the nineteenth century, and in all but the grandest houses, the principal source of light at night was from the fire. Supplementary lighting was provided by rushlights, candles or lamps, most of them supported by holders of wrought, sheet and sometimes cast iron. Rushlights were the cheapest and plainest, made by dipping dried and peeled rushes in melted fat and then drying them. Simple rushlight holders held these clamped steady at about a 30-degree angle; the rush had to be moved up every few minutes and lasted only about half an hour (fig. 142). Candles were a much more expensive alternative, made with wicks of rush or cotton dipped into melted beeswax. Medieval candlesticks consisted of spikes or prickets on which candles were impaled, but by the fifteenth century these were superseded by the socket-type of holder, often adjustable in height by means of movable handles (fig. 144). Floor candlesticks, sometimes very ornate, allowed light to fall over a much wider area and were probably used from the Middle Ages in large houses and churches. Candelabra were designed to hold many candles.

Candles supported in wall-brackets, also known as sconces, appear from the Middle Ages. By the seventeenth century they were more commonly made of brass, but fine eighteenth-century wrought iron examples are known from Italy (fig. 147) and Germany, embellished with gilding and sometimes porcelain mounts. Simpler sheet iron examples appear in eighteenth and nineteenth-century Germany, Scandinavia and North America. Chandeliers, suspended from the ceiling and able to hold up to two dozen candles, were used only in the largest buildings and were more often made of brass than iron. However there is at least one fifteenth-century gilt-iron example, probably German, now in the V&A, and Britain's late nineteenth-century Arts and Crafts Movement inspired some fine wrought iron designs (fig. 145). The iron rods from which these chandeliers hung could be very ornate, as is the late seventeenth-century piece from the church of St Michael, Queenhythe, London (fig. 146).

Oil lamps were one of the oldest forms of lighting. At their simplest all that was needed was a floating wick and a container for the oil (usually from fish). Early examples often consisted of a plain iron dish with a spout at the front for the wick, and another dish beneath to catch the drips. Additional features included a suspension-hook or a stand (fig. 140). Called crusies in Britain, crassets in the Channel Islands and Betty or Phoebe lamps in North America, these lamps were widely used until the nineteenth century, and their design may go back to the the Middle Ages. Being undecorated and of fairly uniform shape, they are impossible to date precisely. More sophisticated oil lamps included the Argand lamp, perfected c.1780–4. This burnt vegetable oil, often contained in a decorative base of cast or sheet iron. In America paraffin became cheaply available from about 1860, and its use here and in Europe for lighting, well into the twentieth century, led to the production of a variety of paraffin-lamp bases in cast iron. But the revolution in lighting, and the fixtures for it, was brought about by the discoveries of gas and electricity. By the 1850s city houses, churches and public buildings could be lit by gas, and gasoliers were of brass or cast iron or were like those of 1869 made for the V&A. By the 1880s lighting by electricity – cleaner and safer – was possible, and a number of early fittings were in wrought iron (figs 68 and 145), if not brass or copper. In the twentieth century, although iron continued to be popular, electric light fittings have rarely been of decorative iron, an unusual example being the wall-light of about 1930 by Edgar Brandt (1880–1960; fig. 148).

141. Hanging lantern for candles and balustrades; wrought iron. German, c.1750, in Schloss Brühl, Germany.

140 (opposite). Crusie lamp; wrought iron. British, eighteenth century (?). The upper pan would have held the oil and the wick, the lower was to catch the oil drips; the hook allowed it to be suspended at will. 566-1891.

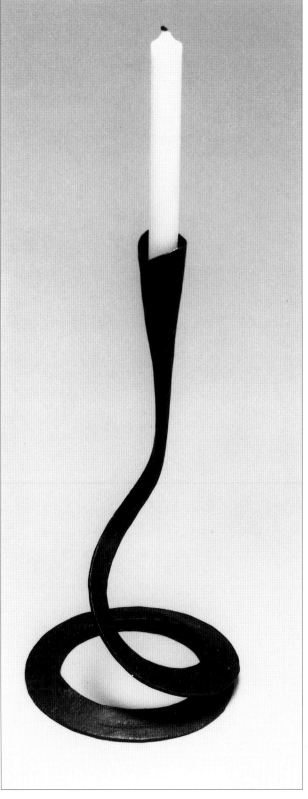

142 (above left). Rushlight holder; wrought iron. English, eighteenth century. M 383-1917.

(above right). Rushlight holder; wrought iron, engraved. Italian, seventeenth century. 1038-1893.

143 (right). Candlestick; wrought iron, by Jan Dudesek. Swiss, 1980. Private collection.

144 (left). Wrought iron. German, dated 1672. Inscribed 'Got geb uns ewige liecht' ('May God give us a little light'). 674-1872.

145 (opposite). Designs for electric chandeliers in wrought iron for St Mary's Episcopal Cathedral, Edinburgh, by the Scottish architect Hippolyte Blanc (1844–1917), c.1880. Ink and colour wash. London, RIBA, British Architectural Library. (RIBA.)

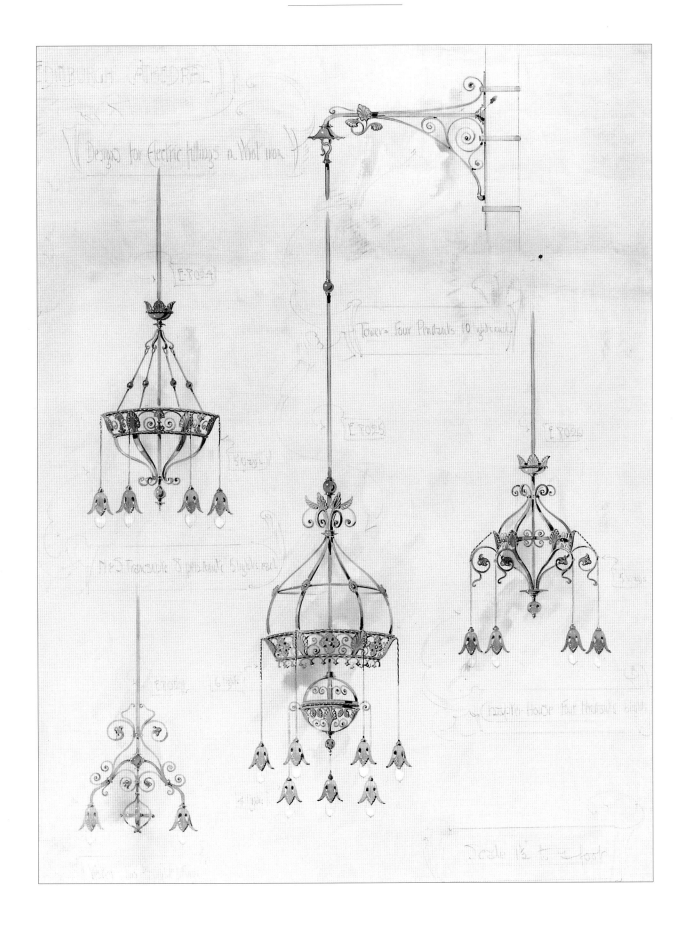

146. Chandelier suspension-rod; wrought iron with original paint and gilding. English, *c.*1700, from the church of St Michael, Queenhythe, London. Such elaborate rods, linked together, allowed lights to be hung from great heights. 876-1868.

147 Pair of wall-lights for
candles; iron, wrought and
gilded. Italian?, mid-
eighteenth century. 1550 and
1551–1856.

148. Wall-light; wrought iron,
by Edgar Brandt. French,
c.1930. Circ 264-1971.

LIGHTING OUTDOORS

Nightfall imposed very real curbs upon social activity until well into the nineteenth century. The brilliant street lighting found today even in small villages was then unknown; since about 1800, the advent of first gas and then electricity has transformed lighting. The two principal types of outside lighting – fixed and portable – have long relied on iron for their supports or containers. Street lighting evolved from the lights put out by house-holders to celebrate church festivals or state events in the Middle Ages.

The earliest recorded street lights, known as cressets, took the form of decorative iron baskets which were fixed on to the walls of some Italian palaces (fig. 149). The best surviving example was made by Nicolò Grosso in 1489 for the Strozzi Palace, Florence and, since the nineteenth century, this has been much imitated. Light came from coils of rope, soaked in pitch, which were placed in the cressets and lit. Throughout Europe for many centuries street lighting was provided by the individual citizen, sometimes impelled by the law. One fifteenth-century Mayor of London, Henry Barton, ordered 'lanthorns with lights to be hanged out on winter evenings', but it was another 300 years before any European city was regularly lit.

Paris in 1666 was first to organize centrally the compulsory hanging out of lanterns at night, and in 1735 the City of Westminster, London, was first to undertake street lighting on every night of the year. Wrought iron lamp-holders were soon to be found in many squares and streets in London, Bath, and Dublin, usually designed as an integral part of the railings of a building (figs 73, 150, 151, 155, 156 and 160). The oil lamp was fitted into the cradle at the top of the lamp-holder, and lit by a burning torch. Torches were extinguished using the iron funnel-shaped snuffer below the lamp (fig. 156).

But such lighting was feeble; walking safely at night became possible only in the nineteenth century with the advent of gas lighting, introduced to the streets of London and Paris soon after 1800. London led the way, with gas lighting in Pall Mall in 1807; by 1823 there were 40,000 gas lamps installed in London streets, their cast iron lamp-posts in a medley of designs (figs 151 and 157). By 1840 gas lamps were also installed in the streets of

149 (left). Cresset or lantern; wrought iron. Italian, sixteenth century. 7802-1862.

150 (right). Lamp-lighter, 1805. The oil lamp is here about to be replaced in its supporting cradle, protected by an iron lid and a glass hemisphere which rests in the circular lamp-holder. Lithograph from William Pyne's *Costume of Great Britain.*

PLATE XXX

PIERS AND LAMPS FOR GATES, AND PALISADE FENCES.

151. Designs for oil and gas lamps in cast iron, 1823. Lamps of the left-hand design, modified for electricity, are still in use in Regent's Park, London. Engraving from L. N. Cottingham, *Smith's and Founder's Director*.

Paris, Berlin, Hanover, Vienna and Leipzig. The many thousands of cast iron standards that were needed gave manufacturers wonderful design and sales opportunities, and their names are often found cast into the bases of surviving examples.

North America led the way in installing electric street lighting, which gave a more intense light, and 90,000 electric street lamps were in place all over the country by 1884. In much of Europe gas did not yield to electricity until well into the twentieth century, and in a few places, like some of London's parks, gas still prevails. Standards for electric lamps were designed to be taller and thinner than for gas, but at first were still of decorative cast iron.

Sometimes the lamps were integrated into other architectural features, as with the lamp-posts by Hector Guimard (1867–1942) which form part of his Art Nouveau schema for Parisian Metro stations. In the course of the twentieth century, street lighting design has generally deteriorated, either into a crude functionalism, often in concrete, or into 'heritage repro'. Increasingly found in Britain's conservation areas, this distressing genre is often adorned with cheap gold paint, as if to emphasize its design deficiency.

Portable lights were lit by candles or oil. These lanterns were generally made of a thin and light sheet iron and were often decoratively pierced, painted or embossed (figs 152 and 153). They could be carried by hand, on poles, attached to carriages or even ingeniously strapped to a messenger's leg (fig. 154). With the advent of electricity they have become redundant.

152 (far left). Lantern for a candle; sheet iron, pierced, stamped and painted. Italian(?), seventeenth century, to be carried on top of a pole to cast extra light. 663-1890.

153 (left). Lantern; sheet iron, pierced and stamped. English or French, c.1800; two candle-holders are visible at the base. M 293-1975.

154 'Miles's patent' designs for oil lamps in pierced sheet iron. English, c.1800. Engraving in contemporary catalogue.

155 Lamp-holders for oil lamps, outside 13 John Adam Street, Adelphi, London (demolished 1937); wrought iron, designed by the architect Robert Adam, c.1768. The stylized Neo-classical 'heart and honeysuckle' motifs on the supports were often used by Adam. M 160-1941. (RCHM.)

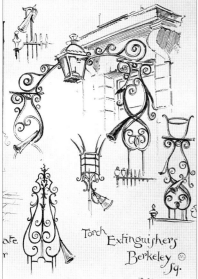

156 (above). Different styles of London eighteenth-century lamp-holders; wrought iron. The funnel-shaped attachments are snuffers used by torchbearers and lamplighters to extinguish their torches. Pen and ink drawing. D 2108-1900.

157 (far left). Gas lamp outside St James's Palace, London; cast iron, probably by T. Edge, dated 1823, with the royal cypher of King George IV. (Author.)

158 (left). Lamp-post outside the Law Courts, London; cast iron, made by Macfarlane of Glasgow, *c.*1882, originally for gas, though now converted to electricity. (Author.)

159 (below). Lanterns; wrought iron. Italian, *c.*1911, designed, like the building at 26 Borgo Ognissanti, Florence, by the architect G. Michelazzi. (Conway Library, Courtauld Institute of Art.)

160 (opposite). Lamps in Torquay, Devon; cast iron, *c.*1910. (John Gay.)

FURNITURE

Iron may seem an uncomfortable material for furniture, yet it has been used for centuries, at first for luxury items of domestic furniture, and in the nineteenth century to furnish gardens and public spaces as well as the home. A very rare early medieval piece, possibly of German or Italian origin, is a folding stool, made of iron inlaid with copper and silver, with bronze decoration (fig. 162). Another rare German work is an ornate chair, now owned by the Earl of Radnor, but for long housed in the Prague Palace Treasure Chamber of the Holy Emperor Rudolf II (r. 1576–1612). Dating from 1574, it is a unique work of craftsmanship in wrought and chiselled iron by the Dresdener Thomas Rucker (c. 1532–1606), a specialist maker of sword hilts and blades, and is decorated with over 120 sculptural reliefs in a Mannerist style. The sixteenth-century Italians were also active in the field; the specialist armourers of Milan also produced plaques to decorate furniture. Sheet iron was embossed with designs and damascened (inlaid) with further patterns in gold and silver.

In the eighteenth century the Russian tsar's specialist armourers made luxury furniture as a sideline at the Imperial Arms Factory at Tula, near Moscow, particularly during the reign of Catherine the Great (1762–96). Tables, chairs and mirrors were produced, made of steel, blued or burnished and embellished with copper, brass or cut steel ornaments. Pieces that once furnished the old imperial palace at Gatchina are now in the Hermitage Museum, St Petersburg; folding armchairs, inlaid with gold and silver, are now in the V&A (fig. 161) and the Musée de l'Armée, Paris.

The growing importance of gardens to late eighteenth-century sensibilities led to a demand for furniture, sometimes of iron, for gardens and, later, conservatories. At first the furniture was in wrought iron, as is the garden chair of the early 19th century (fig. 164), which though graceful is of laboured construction, and might more easily have been cast. Only from the 1830s did cast iron furniture generally become popular. To the progressively minded, cast iron commended itself as a modern material, while to the pragmatic it was attractive because of its robustness and relative cheapness. Elaborate carving and ornament could be produced much more economically in iron than in wood, and then painted to imitate it or bronze. The architect K. F. Schinkel (1781–1841) in the 1820s designed various chairs (fig. 163) for the imperial palace gardens at Potsdam and Berlin, for casting by the Prussian Royal Foundry, Berlin, where they remained in production until the 1860s. Garden furniture inspired pleasing designs, often appropriately taken from plants (figs 167 and 169) and flowers. In Britain the Coalbrookdale Company of Ironbridge came to dominate the market, exporting pieces all over the world.

Such furniture was generally a sideline of stove and grate manufacturers, although a great variety of domestic iron furniture was also made. Cast iron bedsteads, introduced in the 1830s, were popular for hygienic reasons: unlike wood, iron could not harbour bed bugs (fig. 170). Tubular iron rocking chairs were made from about 1840 (fig. 168) and at first were associated with health: an 1845 American encyclopedia described them as being useful for exercise. A riot of tables, chairs, hat-stands and door-stops were made from about 1830 to 1880, the period of major production. Eventually new fashions and the indestructibility of the products killed the market.

Innovative iron furniture design in the twentieth century has until very recently been rare. Most garden furniture is 'heritage repro', copies or pastiches of nineteenth-century models. Exceptions include the Italian wire garden furniture of the 1950s, cast iron benches by Edward Bawden (1903–89), and wrought iron plant-stands of the 1980s by David Watkins (b. 1940) and Albert Paley.

161. Folding chair; steel inlaid with gold. Russian (Tula), c.1750. 1387-1888.

162. Folding stool; iron, inlaid
with copper and silver.
German or Italian, eleventh
century (?). 696-1904.

164. Garden chair; wrought iron, originally painted dark green. English, early nineteenth century. W 11-1977.

163. Garden chair; cast iron painted matt black, designed by K. F. Schinkel, maker unknown. German, c.1825. Examples of this Neo-classical design were made until the 1860s, often painted black.

165. Railway station bench at Thirsk, Yorks; cast iron. English, c.1880, in the 'style of Kensington', according to John Ruskin, *Fors Clavigera*, 1875. (J. Gay.)

166. Bench on the Victoria Embankment, London; cast iron, made by J. D. Berry of London, c.1869–70. (John Gay.)

167. Garden seat; cast iron. English, made by Coalbrookdale & Co., Shropshire, c.1860. Known as the 'Medallion' pattern, it was originally painted brownish to imitate bronze or green for patinated bronze, popular colours for garden furniture. M 6-1979.

169. Plant-stand; cast iron design by Coalbrookdale, Shropshire, c.1860. Engraving from contemporary Coalbrookdale catalogue.

168. Trade-card of John Porter, London, 1840, showing wirework furniture and plant-stands. The tubular rocking chair design remained popular for 20 years and inspired bentwood manufacturers. Engraving.

170. Engraving of a bed in cast iron, made by Peyton of Birmingham. English, 1862. Engraving from the Art Journal, 1862.

LOCKS AND KEYS

Securing valuables is by no means a modern preoccupation. Keys have often been seen as symbols of wealth and power; part of the formal ceremony of surrender has always included the handing over of the keys to a city or fortress. In many cultures keys are also imbued with religious significance: St Peter, for example, is generally depicted with a large key, the symbol to Christians of his power to open the gates of Heaven (fig. 118).

Types of lock and key mechanisms and the degree of decoration have varied greatly over the centuries, from the plain functionalism of the early Middle Ages and the twentieth century to the ornate styles fashionable between the fourteenth and nineteenth centuries. Decoration focused on the key's handle, known as the 'bow', and on the lock-case, and allowed the locksmith to display virtuoso ingenuity and skill, but added nothing to the security of the lock. For that, the important part of a key is in the 'bit', the lower projecting tongue which operates the mechanism (the 'wards') of the lock, allowing it to open or shut. The clefts and holes cut into the bit have to be a perfect match to those in the wards.

Although warded locks are easy to pick, the majority of locks and keys from the Middle Ages until the nineteenth century had this type of mechanism. Extra security was sometimes given by boring the stem of the key into a certain shape, and fitting the lock with a pin to correspond, so that a perfect match was necessary for lock and key to work. Another device was to give the keyhole a distinctive shape, so that the insertion of the wrong key was impossible. Sometimes locks were fitted with mechanisms which injured or trapped the would be lock-picker.

Two basic types of keys were made from the Middle Ages until the nineteenth century: keys with solid stems and keys with hollow tubular stems. The solid-stemmed were usually for door-locks attached to the surface of a door (figs 173, 176 and 177) and could be used

from either side of the lock. The key's bit had to be symmetrical, however complex the clefts, in order to work from either side of the lock. Hollow-stemmed keys could work from only one side of the lock, whether on a door or, more commonly, a chest: the spindle set into the lock had to engage with the key stem.

Locks and keys of varying sophistication are known from ancient Egypt, Greece and China. Egyptian locks were generally of wood and worked on a principle similar to that of the modern Yale lock. The Romans generally used bronze for their locks and keys, and the earliest iron locks and keys to be made in any numbers date from the Middle Ages. Medieval locks consisted of simple springs and bolts attached to a flat plate with an undecorated lock-case; keys were plain. In the eleventh and twelfth centuries they were distinguished by large looped handles, and numbers have been excavated at Winchester, Norwich and Bury St Edmunds in England. Later in the Middle Ages the key stem was longer, the bow smaller; fifteenth-century bows were commonly shaped as hearts, lozenges, spades or kidneys (fig. 175).

The Gothic style, characterized by architectural motifs – pinnacles, quatrefoils and pierced work – was enthusiastically adopted by fourteenth and fifteenth-century locksmiths. By the sixteenth century, lock mechanisms had become increasingly complicated, with better springs and heavier bolts. From about 1550, Renaissance emphasis on Classical motifs – caryatids and pilasters – inspired the making of finely chiselled and engraved locks, especially in Italy and France, as well as lock-cases adorned with piercing, etching and gilding (fig. 174). Personal monograms and heraldic devices were often used as decoration, and locks began to be signed (fig. 172). Superbly decorative 'masterpiece' locks were the finest products of locksmiths, qualifying them as masters after their long apprenticeship (fig. 171). From the seventeenth century there have survived a few pattern-

171. Lock and key; iron, pierced, engraved and etched.
German, signed by the maker, 'CS', dated 1610. With a
mechanism as elaborate as its decoration – which includes the
double-headed eagle emblem of the emperor – this is a typical
German 'masterpiece' lock, the key-hole concealed beneath
the polygonal boss. 2409-1856.

books, with designs that for the first time circulated
widely amongst workshops; they show elaborate lock-
plates as well as keys.

Iron padlocks, to shackle people and animals as well as
objects, go back to the Iron Age. Generally of box shape,
with a keyhole and a hasp, they are often undecorated
and thus hard to date. Their locking mechanism might
be activated by secret combinations of numbers or
letters, or by the release of buttons or studs, as in a
German seventeenth-century puzzle padlock (fig. 178).

From about 1600, England and France were notable
producers of fine locks and keys. English keys were
characterized by turned or fluted stems and bows incorporating slender C scrolls, the French by bows
incorporating sphinxes or dolphins nose to nose (fig.
175). Occasionally English keys are engraved with details

of the park or apartment to which they gave access, or
with their owner's name (fig. 181). Gilt brass was
increasingly used for lock-cases from about 1650, often
combined by the English with steel, pierced and blued.
After 1722 French locksmiths began making locks of
finely cast 'soft' iron, often gilded, to rival those in gilt
brass. Rococo and Neo-classical styles influenced the
decoration of eighteenth-century locks, and keys were
delicately chiselled and pierced, to complement the
ornate cabinets then fashionable.

From about 1800 a plainer, simpler latch-key developed (fig. 175), the direct ancestor of the modern house
key. In the nineteenth century technical improvements in
lockmaking coincided with a revival of Gothic and
Renaissance styles, from about 1820 to the 1880s.
Locksmiths produced especially fine work for the international exhibitions of the 1850s and 1860s (fig. 180). By
about 1900 fashion was turning against ornateness in
locks and keys and focusing upon their mechanisms, and
this emphasis has characterized the twentieth century.

172. Lock and bolt on the Scaliger tomb-grille, Verona; wrought iron. Italian, made by Bovinio di Campilione, c.1380. This type of lock was also used on doors. Here the lock and grille are decorated with the family crest, a ladder (in Italian: *scala*), a pun on their name. (Author.)

173. Lock in St George's Chapel, Windsor, on the north choir aisle door; chiselled iron. English, c.1500. It is rare to find medieval locks still in place. (RCHME.)

174. Lock and key; iron, pierced, chiselled and engraved, by Gaspard Mazelin. French, dated 1649. Its decoration is typical of French Renaissance ornament. From the Bernal Collection. 2066-1855.

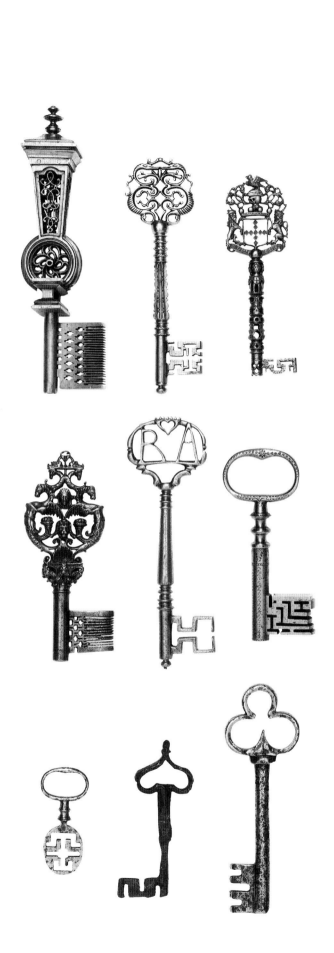

175 (left). Keys.
(top row, left to right):
(a) Steel, chiselled. French,
late seventeenth century.
2295-1855.
(b) Steel, chiselled. English,
seventeenth century.
1368-1900.
(c) Steel, chiselled. English,
late seventeenth century, with
the arms of Ralph Stawell, first
Baron Somerton (cr. 1682).
152-1883.
(centre row, left to right):
(d) Steel, pierced and
chiselled. French, c.1600.
M 646-1910.
(e) Steel, chiselled. English,
dated 1669, engraved with the
name of Sir Robert Abdy of
Albins, Essex. M 36-1929.
(f) Steel, punched with
decoration. English,
eighteenth century. 691-1902.

(bottom row, left to right):
(g) Latch-key, steel. English,
nineteenth century.
M 340-1917.
(h) Wrought iron. English,
fifteenth century. 429-1902.
(i) Iron, chiselled. English,
fifteenth century. M 117-1909.

176 (above). Keys with original
key thongs; wrought iron and
leather. English, c.1400, from
New College, Oxford. The
two larger were for doors, the
smaller for a casket. New
College, founded in 1379, still
possesses ancient chests
which held plate and
documents; the chest
containing the Founder's silver
crozier was fastened with
eight different keys. (C. Blair.)

177 (left). Lock and key on a door in the Long Gallery, Hardwick Hall, Yorks; iron, pierced and engraved. English, c.1700.

178 (below left). Puzzle padlock; steel. German, seventeenth century. If the studs on the face of the padlock are correctly arranged, the steel hands holding the key will rise up and release it. Two turns of the key are necessary to lock or unlock, and in each unlocking an indicator at the back moves forward one point on a circular dial. If, in locking, the key is turned three times, unlocking becomes impossible until a certain knob is correctly turned and pulled. M 8-1932.

179 (below). Griffin-shaped key-escutcheon; iron, pierced and engraved. German, seventeenth century. M 161-1925.

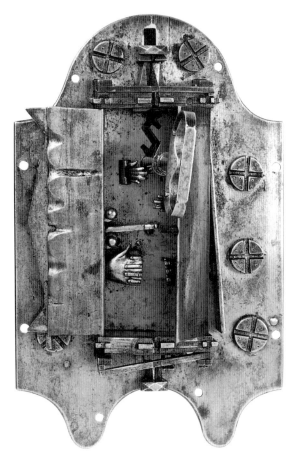

180 (right). Locks and keys in steel, engraved and embellished with brass. English, *c.*1862, made by the firms of Chubb of London and Gibbs & Price of Wolverhampton. Lithograph from J. B. Waring, *Masterpieces of the 1862 Exhibition,* London 1863.

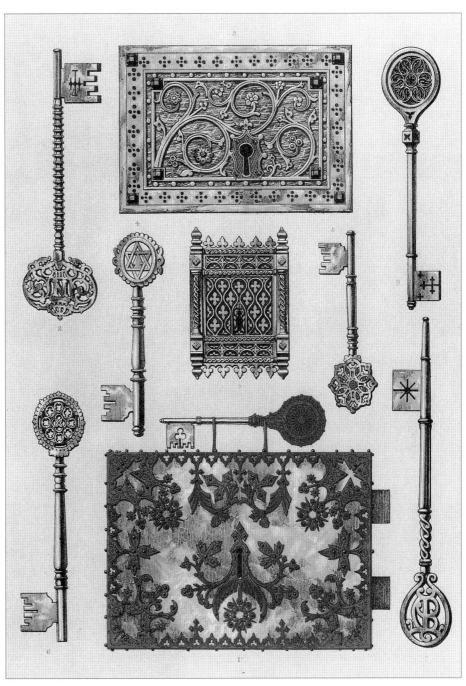

181. Keys
(left). Pass-key; engraved steel. English, *c.*1660, double-ended; the two bits open different locks. Inscribed 'Lord Wentworth', probably for Thomas, 5th Baron (1613–65), Gentleman of the Bedchamber to Charles II. The key was probably for one of the royal chambers. M 5-1964.

(right). Steel, pierced and chiselled, enriched with brass. English, *c.*1660–80. The crowned monogram 'DC' (?) in the bow and the crown motifs on the shank may indicate royal ownership. M 651-1910.

CHESTS, SAFES AND CASKETS

182. Interior view of the Bank of England, with iron strong box;
engraving, c.1695. London, Bank of England Museum.
(The Governor of the Bank of England.)

From the Middle Ages until around 1700, large chests, for storage and seating, were the commonest pieces of furniture in any household. Before the establishment of banks in the seventeenth century chests had also to serve as safes, suitably reinforced with iron straps and formidable locks. Within the home, a chest might store clothing and bedding, documents and jewellery (fig. 185), and gold and silver plate and coin. Institutions and churches also used chests to hold valuables, including documents and parish records. A number of these chests have survived, especially in Britain, Scandinavia and south Germany, and some can still be seen in the places for which they were made. For centuries chests also served as luggage in which travellers transported their possessions. Large chests were usually made of wooden planks, fortified by plain iron bands, and sometimes reinforced with elaborate locks and hingework that might cover much of the surface, acting as decoration as well as protection (figs 183 and 187).

The term 'Armada Chest' describes a distinctive and common type of wrought iron coffer strengthened with interlaced iron bands (fig. 183). In most examples an elaborately engraved lock occupies the whole interior of the lid, with eight bolts that are caught under the in-turned side edges. There is often an imitation keyhole on the front of the chest, the real one being concealed in the lid, and sometimes two or more staples for padlocks. The paint originally decorating most chests rarely survives. The name 'Armada' chest probably arose in the nineteenth century from the romantic but mistaken belief that these chests held bullion to finance the Spanish Armada of 1588, or that they came from wrecked ships. The forerunners of the modern steel safe, they vary in size from a few inches for jewellery, to 5 or 6 feet ($1\frac{1}{2}$ or nearly 2 metres) in length for a banker's reserve. Large numbers were made in southern Germany, particularly in Nuremberg, from about 1580 to 1775, and were exported to all parts of Europe. One such chest, still in the Bank of England, served from at least 1700 to hold bullion (fig. 182). Small chests or coffers (fig. 185) might be made of iron, or of wood, leather or even ivory, reinforced with iron hinges. A popular type from Nuremberg, made between about 1550 and 1700, consisted of steel plaques riveted together and decorated with etched figures and foliage.

From the eighteenth century onwards, wooden chests became plainer, and iron played little part in their decoration. Cast iron, however, being strong, heavy and relatively fire proof, was popular for safes in the nineteenth century. Sometimes relatively plain, these could also be adorned with fashionable motifs, whether Gothic or Neo-classical (fig.186).

183. 'Armada' chest; wrought iron, with original colours; the single lock of steel, engraved. German, c.1600; probably used for bullion. 4211–1856.

184 (left). Detail from the Lady and the Unicorn Tapestries. France c.1484–1500. Paris, Musée de Cluny.

185 (above). Coffers for jewellery and valuables. Top row:
(a) Wrought iron, backed with red cloth. French, fifteenth century. M 640-1910.
(b) Steel openwork, backed with dyed tortoiseshell. Russian, seventeenth century. 48-1869.
(c) Steel, etched with figures. German, seventeenth century. 744-1893.
(d) Cuir bouilli (leather cut and stamped) with wrought iron mounts. Spanish or French, fifteenth century. 4318-1857.
(e) Cast iron openwork. German, early nineteenth century. Known as 'Berlin iron', a type of very fine casting produced by the Prussian Royal Foundry in Berlin, founded in 1804. M 195-1935.
(f) Wrought iron. French?, fifteenth century. M 248-1912.

186 (below). Coffer; cast iron. German, c.1810–30, probably cast in the royal foundry at Gleiwitz. Nuremberg, Germanisches Nationalmuseum, inv. HG 8945.

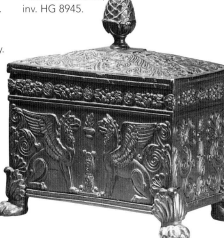

187. Chest; wood with stamped, wrought iron hinges; thought to be from the Abbey of St Denis near Paris, one of the wealthiest abbeys in France. French, thirteenth century. Paris, Musée Carnavalet, 1522 A. (Spadem.)

188. Coffer; wrought iron. Flemish, early sixteenth century. M 295-1912.

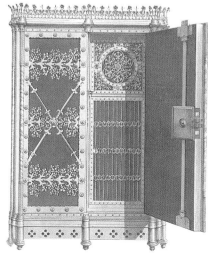

189. Fire-proof safe; wrought iron with red lacquer ground, made by K. Hauschild of Berlin; German, 1862. Lithograph from J. B. Waring, *Masterpieces of the 1862 Exhibition*.

SCREENS, TOMB RAILINGS AND INTERIOR FITTINGS

From the Middle Ages to the present day, the Church has played an important role as patron of ironworkers. Substantial screens and railings were needed to protect the shrines of venerated saints and important tombs from the attentions of over-enthusiastic pilgrims and followers, as well as from thieves. One of the most elaborate grilles – still in place in Westminster Abbey in London – is that around the tomb of Queen Eleanor of Castile (d. 1290; fig. 193), which contrasts with the plainness of the railings around the tomb of the Black Prince (d. 1376) in Canterbury Cathedral and others in Stanton Harcourt Church, Oxon (fig.192), and in Somerset. The design of such railings seems to have provided the model for street railings of the eighteenth and nineteenth centuries.

Iron screens often divided the liturgical spaces in a church (figs 190 and 197). The nave and ambulatory – open to the laity – were separated from the choir – reserved for the clergy. Side chapels were also often secured by iron gates. The style of these screens reflects their period and region of origin; the most widely used motif was a cross. The presence of a skull in a characteristically German chapel gate (fig. 199) suggests that it secured a funerary chapel.

Church interiors are often embellished with other iron furnishings: fonts containing consecrated water needed to be secured with covers. That made by Robert Bakewell in 1718 for St Werburgh's Church, Derby, is exceptional in being entirely made of iron (fig. 195). Wall-niches housing the sacraments or church plate were closed with small iron grilles known as aumbry doors. Iron lecterns to support the Bible or the Psalter were occasionally made by French and Spanish smiths (fig. 191). A few English churches still retain their seventeenth and eighteenth-century stands for hour-glasses; these enabled the preacher to time his sermon at a period when watches were rare (fig. 196). Also still in place, especially in City of London churches, are the ornate stands, often from

the eighteenth century, made to hold a ceremonial mace or sword, the civic symbol of office of a mayor (fig. 198).

Although much ecclesiastical ironwork has survived, it has also inevitably been the victim of changing liturgical fashion. In the Roman Catholic regions of Europe – Spain, Italy and south Germany – much remained *in situ* until recent times. In Protestant northern Europe, both the Reformation in the sixteenth century and the modernizing movements of the nineteenth century resulted in considerable losses, although some pieces were rescued by collectors or museums (fig. 197).

190 (opposite). Choir screen in the Klosterkirche, Einsiedeln, Switzerland; wrought iron. Swiss, seventeenth century. The use of perspective panels was a speciality of Swiss and south German smiths at this date. (Rud. Suter AG, Oberrieden/Zurich.)

191. Lectern; wrought iron. French c.1700, probably from the monastery of La Chaussée Saint-Leu, Amiens. Designed to swivel, it is inscribed 'IHS' (Jesus). Rouen, Musée le Secq des Tournelles. (Author.)

192 (left). Effigy and railings of the tomb, thought to be of Maud, Lady Harcourt; the railings wrought iron. English, c.1400. Decorative fleur-de-lys finials were used from the twelfth century. Stanton Harcourt Church, Oxon.

194 (opposite). Chapel gates; wrought iron. Italian, seventeenth century. 619 & a-1875.

193 (bottom left). Effigy and grille of Queen Eleanor of Castile, the grille wrought and stamped iron, 1292–3, by Thomas de Leghtune (fl. 1280s-90s). One of the most elaborate surviving medieval tomb grilles. London, Westminster Abbey. (RCHM.)

195 (above). Font cover, made for St Werburgh's Church, Derby; wrought and embossed iron, by Robert Bakewell (1682–1752) in 1718. The only surviving font cover entirely of iron and a masterpiece of embossing. (C. Blair.)

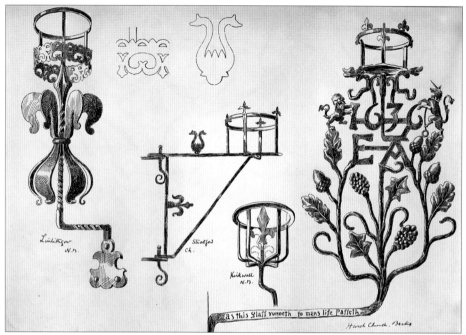

196. Hour-glass stands in wrought iron. British, seventeenth and eighteenth centuries. Common from the Reformation up to around 1800, these held an hour-glass close to the pulpit. The preacher announced his text, reversed the glass, and talked until the sand ran out. Pen and ink drawing. E 385-1911.

198 (below). Ceremonial sword-rest; wrought iron with original paint and gilding. English, c.1816–37. Under the crown are the royal arms and those of the City of London, the London Plaisterers' Company and of Thomas Kelly, Lord Mayor of London in 1836. From an unknown City church. 383-1896.

197. Choir screen from Hereford Cathedral in wrought and cast iron, with wood, copper, brass and mosaic, designed by George G. Scott (1811–78), made by Skidmore & Co., Coventry, 1862. Dismantled in 1967 and now in the V&A, at 36 feet in width this was one of the most monumental of nineteenth-century metal screens. Engraving from The Builder, 1863. M 251-1984.

199. Chapel gate; wrought iron. German seventeenth century. The skull suggests that this was for a funerary chapel. 213-1887.

CROSSES AND TOMB-MARKERS

Iron crosses have marked buildings and the landscape for centuries (fig. 202). By the fifteenth century, Belgian and northern German church spires were often crowned with a cross (fig. 203). In the sixteenth century, Spanish smiths were making ornately embossed processional crosses (fig. 201), and from the seventeenth century Austria and southern Germany used wrought iron crosses as grave-markers. Wrought iron grave crosses of this type were also made in the nineteenth century in North America, in areas like North Dakota that had strong Germanic roots.

200. Grave-slab to Anne Forster; cast iron. English, dated 1591. An early cast memorial, showing the deceased wrapped in a shroud, and the family coats of arms. In Crowhurst Church, Surrey. Drawing by J. L. André.

Grave crosses, often proclaiming the identity of the deceased on attached plaques, continue to be made today in parts of Germany, Austria and Switzerland (fig. 206). In Britain and France mass-produced cast iron grave crosses became popular in the nineteenth century, manufactured among others by Macfarlanes of Glasgow and Barbezat of Paris (fig. 205).

Cast iron tomb markers took various other forms. One of the simplest is a slab shape, as on the early example at Crowhurst, Sussex, dated 1591 and decorated with the image of a shrouded body, and the family coats of arms (fig. 200); the inscription is made up of separately carved letters, not quite correctly assembled (the Fs are upside down), suggesting that the founder was illiterate.

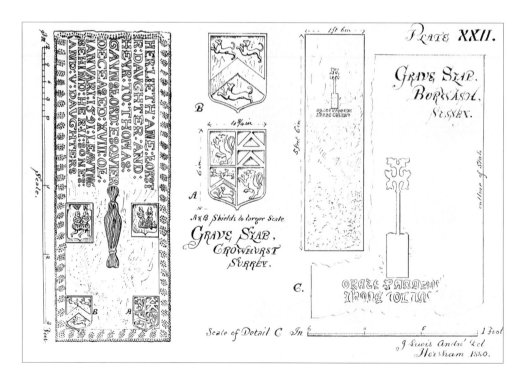

201. Processional cross; wrought iron, embossed, painted and gilt. Spanish c.1550, in the ornate *plateresco* style ('in the manner of a silversmith') typical of Spanish Renaissance ironwork. M 329-1940.

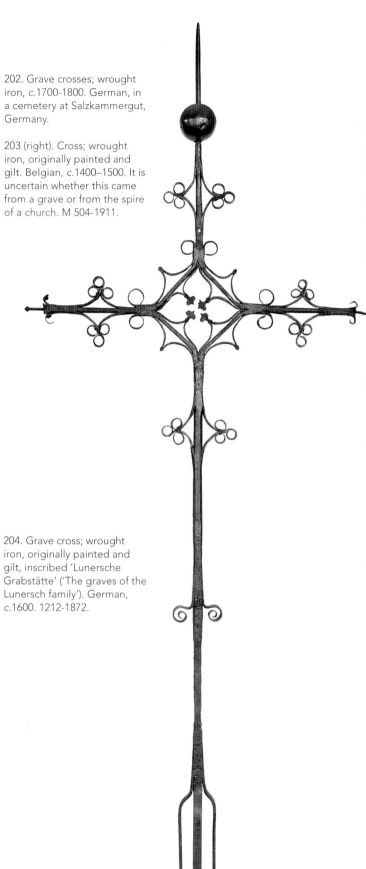

202. Grave crosses; wrought iron, c.1700-1800. German, in a cemetery at Salzkammergut, Germany.

203 (right). Cross; wrought iron, originally painted and gilt. Belgian, c.1400–1500. It is uncertain whether this came from a grave or from the spire of a church. M 504-1911.

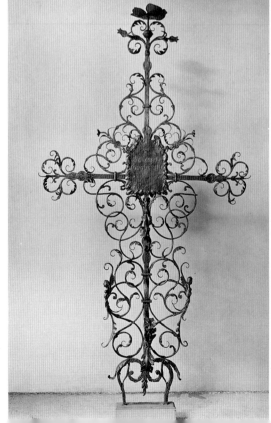

204. Grave cross; wrought iron, originally painted and gilt, inscribed 'Lunersche Grabstätte' ('The graves of the Lunersch family'). German, c.1600. 1212-1872.

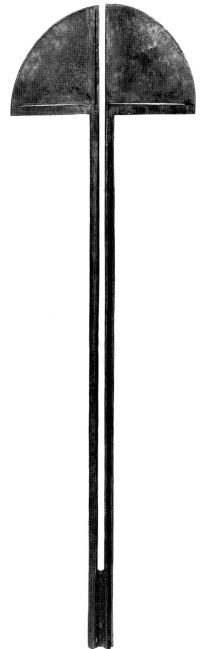

205. Grave crosses in cast iron, by Barbezat & Cie., Paris, 1858. Cast iron crosses generally superseded wrought in the nineteenth century. Engraving from a Barbezat catalogue.

206. Grave cross; wrought cor-ten steel, by Jan Dudesek. Swiss, 1982. Private collection.

DECORATIVE SMALL-SCALE ITEMS

Over the centuries, smiths and then founders have made a great variety of small objects, both functional and decorative, many used in domestic activities like sewing and ironing, eating and drinking. Until the late nineteenth century most clothes for both sexes were normally made at home, as were fine embroidery, lace, tapestry and weaving. Scissors in iron or steel were essential, and were often highly fashioned or decorated (fig. 209). Before the advent of electricity and the standardization of the shape of domestic irons, these could be ornate in form as well as in decoration. Stands or trivets on which to rest the hot irons were especially shaped, and their design offered opportunities for smiths and founders to show off their art. Only the smith could make a wrought trivet with

such personal touches as the initials or name of an individual (fig. 208); these were probably wedding presents.

Special implements too were needed for both eating and drinking, and these were often made by smiths. Apart from such obvious and strictly functional items (generally undecorated) as knives, spoons and forks, all sorts of accessories might be made, like the intricate mill for grinding coffee or spices (fig. 210) or the wrought iron corkscrews, which became necessary with the general use of corks for wine bottles in the eighteenth century.

Iron could serve a wealth of other purposes too; one useful function being explored by various smiths today is that of bookends (fig. 207). Nor should fantasy be overlooked in the wonderful 'toys' produced by the Japanese armourers of the nineteenth and early twentieth centuries. These effortlessly combine the highest skills of the smith with the wit and aesthetic power of the artist.

207. Bookends; wrought iron, by John Creed. Scottish, 1995. Private collection. (J. Creed.)

208. Iron rest; wrought iron, pierced. French, c.1800. Rouen, Musée le Secq des Tournelles. (Author.)

209 (right). Iron; wrought iron, engraved. Italian, seventeenth century. 74-1880.

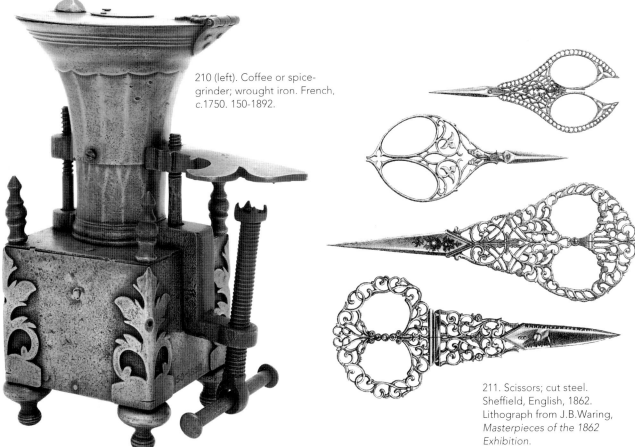

210 (left). Coffee or spice-grinder; wrought iron. French, c.1750. 150-1892.

211. Scissors; cut steel. Sheffield, English, 1862. Lithograph from J.B.Waring, *Masterpieces of the 1862 Exhibition.*

JEWELLERY

Iron and steel are not generally associated with jewellery. Yet the Romans are known to have worn iron finger rings, and jewellery in both iron and steel has enjoyed high fashion status at several different times between the seventeenth century and today. In England the manufacture of cut steel goes back at least to the sixteenth century, and accessories of cut steel were being made at Woodstock near Oxford from about 1600, by screwing or riveting faceted steel studs on to a shaped steel backplate. An alternative method was to link or thread together small faceted beads or sequins made of pierced steel. The strength of steel made it especially suitable for items that received heavy wear, such as buttons, shoe buckles, keys and scissors. In the eighteenth century steel became very fashionable for jewellery, the high polish of the facets imparting to them a diamond-like brilliance (fig. 212). Although of base metal, these pieces were never cheap.

In Britain, as demand grew at home and abroad, workshops were established in Birmingham, London (Clerkenwell) and Wolverhampton. Matthew Boulton of Birmingham (1728–1809) was the first manufacturer to set Wedgwood ceramic plaques in cut steel (fig. 212), thereby extending its aesthetic appeal. During the 1780s,

when 'Anglomania' was in fashion, large quantities of English cut steel were exported to France. By the nineteenth century it was being made there, as well as in Italy, Spain, Prussia and Russia, and it remained popular until about 1900. Marcasites – faceted crystals of iron pyrites – were an alternative to cut steel that were popular in France and Switzerland between about 1750 and 1850.

Jewellery made from finely cast iron, notable for its delicate lacy appearance (fig. 211) was a speciality of the Prussian Royal Foundry, established in Berlin in 1804. Production was promoted by the Prussian War of Liberation fought from 1813 to 1815 against Napoleon and the French. To help finance this struggle, women were encouraged to give their gold wedding rings and other jewellery. In return they received cast iron jewellery, worth little intrinsically, but aesthetically appealing, and sometimes inscribed patriotically 'Gold gab ich für Eisen' ('I gave gold for iron'). The Iron Cross medal, awarded since 1813 for military gallantry, was designed by the architect and designer K. F. Schinkel in 1813 and produced by the Prussian Royal Foundry.

From about 1815 to 1850, 'Berlin iron' jewellery was fashionable throughout Europe. Styles ranged from Gothic to Neo-classical and naturalistic. Casting methods relied on using very pure iron and fine sand for the moulds. As cast iron cannot be soldered, the separate elements were linked with loops. Berlin remained the manufacturing centre and exported widely, but some jewellery was made elsewhere, in parts of Austria, Bohemia, Germany and notably Paris. Here moulds were used that had been taken by the French from Berlin during their occupation of the city in 1806.

The nineteenth-century fondness for experiment led jewellers occasionally to combine iron with other materials, but it is only in the late twentieth century that iron and steel are again being used in significant new forms for the making of jewellery (fig. 213).

212 (opposite). Bracelets; cast iron. German, made in Berlin by the Prussian Royal Foundry, c.1830. The Foundry specialized in producing such small articles as plaques, snuff-boxes and jewellery, work now known as 'Berlin iron'. 32-1888 and Circ. 172-1917

213 (left). Buttons and plaques; cut steel, set with jasper-ware plaques by Wedgwood, and probably made at Matthew Boulton's Soho Works, Birmingham, c.1790. 5818-1853 and 277-1866.

214 (above). Neckpieces; stainless steel, photopierced and etched, hand finished and polished; the centre pieces are interchangeable with the fastenings. Designed and made by Ann Marie Shillito. British, 1972. Private collection.

215 (left). Fan; cast 'Berlin' iron. One of a pair made under the direction of Edward Schott at Ilsenburg-am-Harz to demonstrate the fineness which could be achieved in iron castings. It was shown at the International Exhibition of 1862. 5369-1901.

PART THREE

IRONWORKING PRODUCTION AND TECHNIQUES

1. The metal – definitions

Except in the form of meteorites, pure iron is extremely rare in nature. However, it occurs in abundance as iron ore, a reddish earth from which the metal must be extracted by applying intense heat. Iron is of little practical use until alloyed (combined) with other elements, principally carbon, after which it is highly versatile.

Wrought iron is fairly pure iron, containing some carbon and threads of *slag* (waste) absorbed during the refining process. A light grey colour, it has a pronounced woody grain and can be freely shaped: hammered, bent, split, twisted, cut or stretched, whether hot or cold. The iron becomes harder and more brittle with hammering but annealing (heating and then cooling slowly) returns it to its original state. As its name suggests, wrought iron was the material used by blacksmiths until very recently. It is ductile, strong in tension and relatively rust resistant.

216 (opposite). An iron furnace showing different casting operations. In figs 1 and 2 the sand is being packed into a flask for a closed mould, and in fig. 3 weights are being placed on the flasks (which probably contain several moulds) prior to pouring in the iron. In fig. 4 an open mould is being prepared: a fireback pattern is being pressed face down, into the sand, *c.* 1765. Engraving from Diderot's *Encyclopédie*, Paris, 1765.

217 (above). Coal-hole cover; cast iron, Jones & Co., London, *c.* 1850. Like firebacks, these are one-sided castings, the simplest form. The motif of cannon and balls suggests that these formed a major part of Jones's production. (John Gay.)

Cast or *pig iron* has a high carbon content (2.2%–5%). This makes it hard, and too brittle to be forged – it will shatter if hammered – but allows it to melt readily and to be cast into moulds. Useless to the blacksmith, it is ideal for the mass production of identical objects (fig. 217). It has considerable heat resistance, and is very strong in compression.

Mild steel contains up to 1.5% carbon, and sometimes other elements, but is basically wrought iron with the slag removed. Its appearance lacks the graininess of wrought iron. It can be given greater strength by various heat treatments, and its properties depend on these and on its carbon content. It can be forged or cast, and is today the material commonly used by blacksmiths, while in industry it is used to make such structures as bridges, cars and ships.

Carbon steel (*c.* 0.5–1.5% carbon) is stronger, harder and more resistant to corrosion than iron. It was made in small quantities until the nineteenth century and used mostly for edged tools, weapons and cutlery. Industrial alloy steels introduced in the late twentieth century include such metals as nickel, chromium and tungsten.

2. Production methods

By about 3500 BC the simplest technique of extracting iron from the ore had been mastered. Charcoal heated with iron ore to a temperature of 1200°C produced a *bloom* or lump of iron mixed with impurities. These could then be removed by hand hammering. This technique, known as *direct smelting*, was used in Europe from about 500 BC to AD 1500.

The iron ore and charcoal were placed in alternate layers and ignited, either in furnaces, which at their most primitive consisted of depressions in the ground, or in stone shafts, which soon developed into cupola-shaped furnaces made of fired clay. High temperatures could be achieved by fanning the flames with bellows. Waste products from the ore (*slag*) flowed out of the bottom of the furnace, leaving behind a porous mass of fairly soft iron (*bloom*). This was hammered while hot, to remove as much slag as possible, and was then divided into smaller pieces suitable for subsequent forging. Furnaces gradually increased in size, and in Germany, by *c.* 1350, had assumed what was to be the standard shape of two truncated cones.

The major technological advance of the Middle Ages

218. Blacksmiths at work in an eighteenth-century forge. Smiths are forging a bar at one anvil, tools are scattered near another. On the right a smith heats an iron bar at the forge, the fire's flames fanned by a pair of mechanically powered bellows. Engraving from Diderot's *Encyclopédie*, Paris 1765.

219 (below). Pattern for the front plate of a stove; carved wood. Norwegian, 1782, incorporating the furnace name 'Bolvigswerk' beside the metallurgical symbol for iron. Oslo, Norsk Folkemuseum, no. 1905-358. (Norsk Folkemuseum.)

220 (left). V&A gates in Jim Horrobin's workshop. Forged with a power hammer, the marks of which are visible on the flanges; mild steel, designed and made by J. Horrobin. English, 1982. M 139 & a-1984.

221. Forging iron with a power-hammer. Albert Paley, Rochester, USA, c. 1980. (A. Paley.)

was the blast furnace, which allowed cast iron to be produced for the first time. By about 1400 it was found that waterpower could be harnessed to drive huge bellows; the resulting stronger draught produced a higher temperature. This caused the iron to absorb some carbon from the charcoal fuel, and to become molten. This liquid iron was run off from the furnace, channelled directly into moulds (in the form of firebacks, for example), or into intermediary moulds known as *pigs* and allowed to cool (fig. 216). Purer and forgeable iron, using *pigs* or lumps of cast iron, was produced by smelting and hammering in a *finery*, to remove carbon and other impurities, a process known as the *indirect smelting method*. Pig iron also needs remelting, with scrap iron, to produce cast iron.

During the seventeenth century an increasing shortage of wood, and so charcoal, prompted experiments with an alternative fuel, coal. In 1710 Abraham Darby in Coalbrookdale, Shropshire, made one of the earliest successful attempts, using coal converted into coke. Coke only slowly replaced charcoal as furnace fuel, but by the nineteenth century the widespread use of coke had facilitated an enormous expansion of the iron industry, with relatively low production costs thanks to technological advances.

3. Wrought iron, basic tools and techniques

Wrought iron is forged by the blacksmith on an anvil (fig. 218). From time immemorial the smith's essentials have been a forge in which to heat the iron, a water tank in which to cool it, a hammer, tools and an anvil. Set on

In addition to these, many smiths today use powered tools. The most important is the electric *power-hammer*, with interchangeable top and bottom dies (in effect, hammers and anvils; fig. 221). Although water- and steam-powered hammers have been used since medieval times for large-scale operations, the power-hammer has revolutionised the size, quantity and decoration of the work that a smith can produce single handed (fig. 220). Some smiths have also adopted the oxyacetylene cutter, which has long been used in heavy industry. Its high temperature flame burns the metal locally, and enables the smith to cut substantial thicknesses very quickly – incidentally producing distinctive decorative effects.

The simplest way to join two pieces of iron is to weld them by heating both to a high temperature and hammering them together until they fuse. Other methods include *collaring* (encircling the parts to be joined with small metal collars figs 11, 36 and 38), *mortising* (as in carpentry, fig 12), *riveting* and *screwing*.

Most wrought iron designs consist of an interplay between various forms of scrollwork and straight elements, whether plain, twisted or angled. Techniques used to add decorative variety include:

Blueing: the surface of iron or steel is heated until it glows and is then quenched (plunged in water), when it turns blue, the shade varying according to temperature. The technique is used for both decorative effect and because it helps to inhibit rust (fig. 115).

Carving: the iron is carved cold in exactly the same way as stone or wood (fig. 13), the most difficult way of decorating ironwork.

Chasing: hammering out a pattern on sheet metal from the front using a variety of round-ended tools which produce patterns such as ovals, squares and lines. The technique moves the metal around rather than removing it, as in engraving (fig. 222).

Chiselling: by using a hammer and a steel chisel, iron can be worked like stone or wood; often found on locks and keys (figs 12, 173-5).

Damascening: the art of encrusting gold, silver or copper wire on the surface of iron or steel. A pattern is traced on to the surface of the metal, and finely undercut with a sharp instrument. The wire is then hammered into these minute furrows. This term is derived from Damascus, the city whose early goldsmiths were supposed to have pioneered the technique (fig. 224).

222. Embossed and chased mask from the Fountain Garden screen, Hampton Court, near London: detail of the back; wrought iron, embossed. English, by Jean Tijou, *c.* 1693. Lent by Historic Royal Palaces to the V&A.

223 (opposite). Catalogue showing the wrought and cast products of the Van Dorn Iron Works Co., USA, *c.* 1890. Winterthur (USA), Henry du Pont Library. (Winterthur Library.)

a wooden block which acts as shock absorber, the most common type of anvil has a flat top surface, horn shaped at one end and blunt at the other. It is used as a solid base for hammering the heated iron into shape, for welding and for chiselling, and curved shapes can be made on its pointed end. The blunt end, known as the *heel,* has differently shaped holes, notably the round *pritchel-hole* that simply allows a punch to be driven through iron that is on the anvil, and the rectangular *hardie-hole* that serves to secure various fixed anvil tools. Amongst the most common of these tools are *stakes* (miniature anvils for producing various special shapes in the metal), the *hardie* (a wedge-shaped chisel used for splitting hot metal and for cutting lengths), and *swages* (simple dies with an upper and a lower part, used for the finishing of rods and finials.

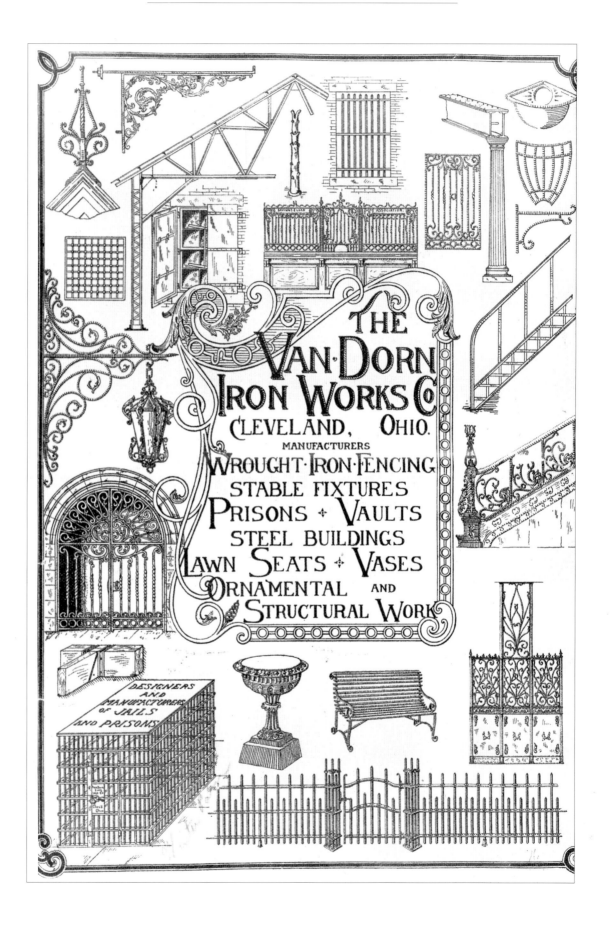

Die: a hardened steel stamp, cut with a design, which, when struck into the surface of hot metal, leaves an impression of the design. The technique was first used in medieval times (fig. 224).

Embossing (or *repoussé* work): the art of raising ornament in relief from the reverse side. The design is first drawn on the flat metal surface and the motifs outlined with a tracer, which transfers the essentials to the back of the plate. This is then embedded face down in an asphalt block and the portions to be raised are hammered down

225 (opposite). Detail of the east door, St George's Chapel, Windsor; wrought iron, stamped and signed by the smith Gilebertus. English *c.* 1240. (RCHME.)

224 (below). Plaque embossed and damascened in gold and silver, showing the biblical story of Judith and Holofernes. Italian (Milanese), *c.* 1550. M663-1910.

into the asphalt. Next the plate is removed and re-embedded with the face uppermost. Hammering is continued, this time forcing the background of the design into the asphalt. A series of these processes is followed finally by chasing (fig. 222).

Engraving and Etching: processes whereby surface designs are produced respectively by using a burin (sharp tool) and by acid (fig. 226).

4. Cast iron

Components essential for producing a piece of cast iron-work were a *pattern*, a *mould*, and the founding or *casting process* itself. The pattern was of wood, plaster of Paris or metal; precision was needed in making it to take account of the shrinkage of cast iron when cold (fig. 219).

The mould was made of different types of sand packed

226. Plaque with 'A'; steel, etched and inlaid with copper and brass; detail of the entrance to the Berlin City Library, by Fritz Kühn. German, 1965.

into an iron frame known as a *flask*. The sand could be *green* (wet) or dry. Two types of mould – open and closed – were used, the former for simple one-sided objects (fig. 217) like firebacks, the latter for complex shapes. Open moulds were often set into the foundry floor, and made of wet sand. The pattern was pounded into the sand with a sledge-hammer, removed, and apertures made in the mould: the *sprue*, through which the molten metal was poured, and *risers*, for the escaping air.

Closed moulds were made up of several parts which fitted together to enclose the iron completely. To minimize weight and cost, complex castings were often hollow; for this a core mould was used – that is, another mould placed inside the closed mould. The metal was heated in a furnace until molten and poured into the moulds. Once cool, the shape of the cast iron was fixed. Unlike cast bronze, which allowed additional chasing and polishing, little more could be done to cast iron, other than to paint it.

5. Surface finishes

Iron normally begins to rust as soon as it is smelted from its ore, and it needs some protection. In the Middle Ages wrought iron was varnished, dipped in pitch, or tinned, as well as sometimes being painted and gilded. In Europe, from *c.* 1600 to 1900, wrought and cast ironwork seem frequently to have been gilded and painted blue, grey, green or white, or given a bronze finish (see figs 15, 21, 147 and 198). It seems that the fashion, still prevalent in Britain and North America, of painting iron black may have begun around 1900. Nowadays other possibilities are to wax it, to galvanize it with zinc and then paint it, or simply to leave it with a layer of rust.

SELECTED READING

Just some of the enormous literature on the subject; most books indicated have good bibliographies.

THE V&A AND ITS COLLECTION

Physick, John, *The Victoria and Albert Museum: The history of its building*, London, 1982.
Somers Cocks, Anna, *The Victoria and Albert Museum: The making of its collection*, London, 1980.

PART 1: BRIEF HISTORY
International Surveys and Contemporary

Fe: An exploration of iron through the senses, British Artists Blacksmiths' touring exhibition, 1994-6.
Ffoulkes, Charles, *Decorative ironwork, from the XIth to the XVIIIth century*, London, 1913. Excellent historical review.
Gardner, J. Starkie, *Ironwork*, London, 1922-30, repr.1978 (3 vols). Still the classic survey, although not all attributions are reliable: illustrated mostly from the V&A collections.
Geerlings, Gerald Kenneth, *Wrought iron in architecture*, New York and London, 1929. Discussion of techniques and excellent illustrations of American and European work.
Hoever, Otto, *A handbook of wrought iron from the Middle Ages to the end of the eighteenth century*, London and New York, 1962. Includes good photos of European gates, grilles, door furniture, fire-irons and signs.
Made of iron, Houston, Texas, University of St Thomas exhibition, 1966.
Robertson, Edward Graeme and Joan, *Cast iron decoration: A world survey*, New York, 1977. An excellent review.
Towards a new iron age, Victoria & Albert Museum exhibition, London 1982. The first international contemporary exhibition in Britain.

GENERAL SURVEY

America

Barnes, Frank, *Hooks, rings and other things: New England ironwork 1660-1860*, Hanover, Mass, 1988.
Bining, Arthur Cecil, *Pennsylvania iron manufacture in the eighteenth century*, Harrisburg, Pennsylvania Historical and Museum Commission, 1979.

Gayle, Margot, and Gillion, Edmund, *Cast iron architecture in New York*, New York, 1974.
Iron solid wrought/USA: The work of American smiths, 1776-1976, Carbondale, Illinois. Southern University of Carbondale exhibition, 1976.
Kauffman, Henry, *Early American ironware, cast and wrought*, Rutland, Vermont, 1966.
Meilach, Dona, *Decorative and sculptural ironwork: Tools, techniques and inspiration*, New York, 1977.
Mulholland, James A., *A history of metals in colonial America*, Alabama, 1981.
Romaine, Lawrence B., *A guide to American trade catalogs, 1744-1900*, New York, 1960.
Sanders, Clyde A., and Gould, C., *History cast in metal*, Cast Metals Institute, American Foundrymen's Society, 1976.
Schiffer, Herbert, Peter and Nancy, *Antique iron: Survey of American and English forms*, Exton, Pennsylvania, 1979.
Simmons, Marc, and Turley, Frank, *Southwestern colonial ironwork*, Santa Fe, 1980.
Sonn, Albert H., *Early American wrought iron*, New York, 1928. Drawings include tools, gates and balconies.
Southworth, Susan and Michael, *Ornamental ironwork*, Boston, USA, 1978. An excellent survey of the design, history and use of cast and wrought iron, particularly in American architecture.
Sturges, W. K., *The origins of cast iron architecture in America*, New York, Da Capo Press, 1970.
Waite, Diana, *Ornamental ironwork: Two centuries of craftsmanship in Albany and Troy*, Albany, 1990.

Australia

Turner, Brian, *Australia's iron lace*, Sydney, 1985.

Belgium

Ffoulkes, Charles, 'Belgian ironwork', *Connoisseur*, vol. 41, London, 1915.

British Isles

Ayrton, Maxwell, and Silcock, Arnold, *Wrought iron and its decorative use*, London, 1929. A history of wrought iron with excellent photos of British work.

Barraclough, K. C., *Sheffield steel*, Sheffield, 1976.

Chatwin, A., *Cheltenham's ornamental ironwork*, Cheltenham, 1974.

—- *Into the new iron age: Modern British blacksmiths*, Cheltenham, 1995.

Cleere, H., and Crossley, D., *The iron industry of the Weald*, Leicester, 1985.

Cottingham, L.N., *The Smith's and Founder's Director, containing a series of designs and patterns for ornamental iron and brass work*, London, 1824. Contains many designs for cast and wrought iron.

Davies, Philip, *Troughs and drinking fountains*, London, 1989.

Edwards, I., *Decorative cast ironwork in Wales*, Gower, 1989.

Gardner, J. Starkie, *English ironwork of the 17th and 18th centuries*, London, 1911, facsimile repr, New York, 1976. The classic account of the best period of English ironwork written by a practising smith.

—- ed., *A new booke of drawings invented and designed by J. Tijou, 1693*, London, 1896.

Gay, J. and Stamp, G., *Cast Iron*, London, 1985.

Geddes, J., 'A Master Smith of the Middle Ages: Thomas of Leighton', *Country Life*, 14 August 1975.

—- 'Iron', in *English medieval industries: Craftsmen, techniques, products*, ed. J. Blair and N. Ramsay, London and Rio Grande, 1991.

Gloag, John, and Bridgwater, Derek, *A history of cast iron in architecture*, London, 1948. Misleadingly entitled for it is one of the best accounts of cast iron, covering all types of object, and well illustrated.

Harris, John, *English decorative ironwork from contemporary source books, 1610-1836*, London, 1960. A selection of drawings from original source books, including Tijou's 'A new booke of drawings'.

Hollister-Shorte, G. J., *Discovering wrought iron*, Tring, 1970. A short but excellent guide. Illustrated.

Jackson-Stops, G., 'English Baroque ironwork' (3 articles), *Country Life*, January and February 1971.

Lindsay, John Seymour, *An anatomy of English wrought iron*, London, 1964. Remarkable drawings of details and techniques.

Lister, Raymond, *Decorative cast ironwork in Great Britain*, London, 1960. Good technical information and useful photos and drawings.

—- *Decorative wrought ironwork in Great Britain*, London, 1957, repr. Newton Abbot, 1970. Very good introduction to tools, materials and techniques, followed by a historical survey.

Murphy, Bailey Scott, *English and Scottish wrought ironwork*, London, 1904.

Parissien, Stephen, *Adam style*, London, 1992.

—- *Regency style*, London, 1992.

—- *Palladian Style*, London, 1992.

Scott, B., *Early Irish ironworking*, Ulster, 1990.

Stamp, Gavin, *Telephone boxes*, London, 1989.

Thorne, Robert, ed., *The iron revolution, architects, engineers and structural innovation, 1780-1880*, London, RIBA, 1990.

Canada

Arthur, Eric, and Richie, Thomas, *Iron*, Toronto, 1982.

Hore, R. E., *History of the iron industry in Canada*, Ottawa, 1925.

Central Europe

Schmuttermeier, Elizabeth, and Ostergard, Derek, eds, *Cast iron from Central Europe, 1800-1850*. Exhibition at the Bard Institute, New York, 1994.

Rasl, Z., *Decorative cast ironwork, catalogue of castings 16th-20th centuries*, Prague, 1980.

France

Blanc, Louis, *Le fer forgé en France aux XVI et XVII siècles*, Paris and Brussels, 1928.

Blanc, Louis, *Le fer forgé en France. La régence: Aurore, apogée, declin*, Paris and Brussels, 1930. Amongst the best surveys of French ironwork.

Clouzot, Henri, *La ferronnerie moderne*, Paris, 1928. Photos of interesting Art Deco ironwork.

Contet, F., *Ferronnerie ancienne au Musée Calvet à Avignon*, Paris, 1926.

D'Allemagne, Henry-René, *Les anciens maitres serruriers et leurs meilleurs travaux*, Paris, 1943. Valuable illustrations.

—- *Ferronnerie ancienne: Catalogue du Musée le Secq des Tournelles*, Paris, 1924.

Faure, Philippe, *La ferronnerie d'art, des origines à nos jours*, Dijon, 1981. Four vols. Detailed drawings. The best up-to-date account.

Frank, Edgar, *Old French ironwork*, Cambridge, Mass, 1950.

Schmid, Charles, *La ferronnerie Française, aux XVII et XVIII siècles; décoration ancienne*, 3 series, Paris, 1909. An excellent reference guide.

Vandour, C., ed., *La ferronnerie*, Métiers d'Art, Paris, 1982.

Germany

Baur-Heinhold, M., *Geschmiedetes-eisen, vom mittelalter bis um XIX*, Königstein im Taunus, 1971.

Kuhn, F., *Wrought iron* (trans. C. B. Johnson), London, 1965.

Roeper, A., and Bosch, H., *Deutsche schmiedearbeiten aus fünf jahrhunderten*, Munich.

Schmidt, Eva, *Der preussische eisenkunstguss*, Berlin, 1981. 18th and 19th century cast iron in N. Germany, including Berlin iron jewellery.

Stuttman, Ferdinand, *Deutsche schmiedeeisen-kunst: I-mittelalter, II-renaissance und-frühbarock*, Munich, 1927.

Italy

Ferrari, Giulio, *Il ferro nell'arte Italiana*, Milan, 2nd ed., 1923. An Italian text illustrated by many of the best examples of Italian craftsmanship.

Thomas, Walter G., and Fallon, John T., *Northern Italian details*, New York, 1916.

Russia

Malchenko, M., *Art objects in steel,* by Tula craftsmen, Leningrad, 1974. Well-illustrated account of the steel furniture produced at Tula.

Spain

Aragones, Maria José, *Hierros Antiguos*, Madrid, 1989.
Byne, A., and Stapley, M., *Rejeria of the Spanish renaissance*, New York, 1914. Still the outstanding book on the subject.
—- *Spanish interiors and furniture,* New York, 1921-25. Excellent for use of iron in interior settings.
—- *Spanish ironwork*, New York 1915.

Sweden

Karlsson, Lennart, *Medieval ironwork in Sweden*, Stockholm, 1988.

INDIVIDUALS

BAKEWELL, Robert
Dunkerley, S., *Robert Bakewell, artist blacksmith*, Cranford, 1988.
BENETTON, Simon
Mangeri, Salvatore, *Simon*, catalogue of an exhibition held at the Galleria d'Arte Moderna San Marco, Bassano del Grappa, February, 1981.
BENETTON, Toni
Mandel, Gabriele, and Bortolato, L. G., *Toni Benetton*, Treviso, 1970.
BERGMEISTER, German and Manfred
Stahl und form, kunstschmiedearbeiten, Dusseldorf, n.d.
BRANDT, Edgar
Essenbrey, Paul, 'Brandt, Master Ironworker, a great French craftsman', *The International Studio*, vol. 80, 1924, pp.253-8.
BUTLER, Reg
Melville, Robert, 'Personages in iron', *Architectural Review*, CVIII, 1951, pp.147-51.
DARBYS
Raistrick, Arthur, *Dynasty of iron founders: The Darbys of Coalbrookdale,* Newton Abbot, 1970. The best account of the pioneering Darbys.
DAVIES Brothers
Edwards, Ifor, *Davies Brothers, Gatesmiths*, Welsh Arts Council, Cardiff, 1977. Exhibition catalogue.
GAUDÌ, Antonio
Guell, Xavier, *Guide Gaudì*, Barcelona, 1991.
GUIMARD, Hector
Thiebaut, Philippe, *Guimard, l'art nouveau*, Paris, 1992.
HORTA, Victor
Borsi, Franco, *Victor Horta*, Brussels, 1970. Illustrations of the work of an important Art Nouveau designer of ironwork.

KÜHN, Fritz
Decorative work in wrought iron and other metals, London, 1967 and 1980. This book consists mainly of photographs and drawings exploring the range of Kühn's work.
LAMOUR, Jean
France-Lanord, Albert, *Jean Lamour, serrurier du roi 1698-1771*, Nancy, 1991.
MACKINTOSH, Charles Rennie
Charles Rennie Mackintosh: Ironwork and metalwork at Glasgow School of Art, selected and described by H. Jefferson Barnes, Glasgow School of Art, 2nd ed. with revisions, 1978.
MAZZUCOTELLI, Alessandro
Bossaglia, Rossana, and Hammacher, Arno, *Mazzucotelli: L'Arista Italiano del ferro battuto liberty*, Milan, 1971. A large-format photographic essay on the work of this important Italian Art Nouveau ironworker.
PALEY, Albert
Lucie-Smith, Edward, *Paley — Art-metal-design*, New York, 1996.
POILLERAT, Gilbert
Baudot, François, *Gilbert Poillerat, maitre ferronnier*, Paris, 1992.
SCHINKEL, Karl Frederich
Snodin, Michael, ed., *Karl Frederich Schinkel*, New Haven and London, 1991.
SUBES, Raymond
Clouzot, Henri, *Raymond Subes, maitre ferronnier, dernières oeuvres*, Paris 1931.
YELLIN, Samuel
Andrews, Jack, *Samuel Yellin*, Ocean City, MD, USA, 1992.
Davis, Myra T., *Sketches in iron: Samuel Yellin, American master of wrought iron, 1885–1940,* Washington DC, Dimock Gallery of the George Washington University, 1971. Exhibition catalogue.

PART 2: FORMS AND FUNCTIONS

For all sections many of the books in Part 1 will be useful.

Iron in Architecture

Baur-Heinhold, M., *Schmiedeeisen gitter, tore und gelander*, Munich, 1977.
Beard, C. R., 'English Medieval and Renaissance closing-rings', *Connoisseur*, February and March, 1928.
Gardner, J. Starkie, *English ironwork of the 17th and 18th centuries*, London, 1911.
Godfrey, W. H., *The English Staircase*, London, 1911.
Hollister-Short, G. J., 'Precursors of the 13th century great hinge', *Connoisseur*, February, 1970.
Jackson, F. N., 'Old door-knockers', *Connoisseur*, XVI, 1906.
Messent, C. J. W., *The old-door knockers of Norwich*, Norwich, 1948.
Parissien, Stephen, *Doors and windows*, London, Georgian Group, 1981.
Streeter, Donald, 'Early wrought iron hardware: Spring latches', *Antiques,* August, 1954.

Iron Outdoors

Bailey, P. F., *Vieilles enseignes de Paris en fer forgés*, Paris, 1925.
Fournier, E., *Histoire des enseignes de Paris*, Paris, 1884.
Fox, Celina, *The battle of the railings*, Architectural Association Files, No. 29, 1995.
Gardner, J. Starkie, *English ironwork of the 17th and 18th centuries*, London, 1911.
Heal, Ambrose, *Sign-boards of old London shops*, London, 1947.
Price, F. G. Hilton, *The signs of Old Lombard Street*, London, 1902.
Stein, Helga, *Woher der wind weht: Windfahnen und wetterhähne*, Hildersheim, 1985.

Domestic Interiors: The Hearth

Allen, J. Romilly, 'Kettle-tilters', *The Reliquary*, vol. VI, 1900.
Caspall, J., *Making fire and light in the home pre-1820*, London, 1987.
Fearn, J., *Domestic bygones*, Tring, 1977.
Feild, R., *Irons in the fire: A history of cooking equipment*, Marlborough, 1984.
Gilbert, Christopher, and Wells-Cole, A., *The fashionable fireplace, 1660-1840*, Leeds, 1985.
Groft, Tammis, *Cast with style — 19th century cast iron stoves from the Albany area*, revised ed., Albany 1984.
Harris, Eileen, *Keeping warm*, London, 1982.
Hildburgh, W. L. 'Wafering-irons – German 16th century', *Proceedings of the Society of Antiquaries*, vol. 26, 1913-14; 'Wafering-irons – Italian 15th-16th centuries', *Proceedings of the Society of Antiquaries*, vol. 27, 1915.
Hollister-Short, G. J., 'Sophisticated cranes', *Connoisseur*, June 1974, pp.116-24.
Kauffman, Henry J., and Bowers, Quentin, *Early American andirons*, Nashville, Tennessee, 1974.
Ladd, Paul R., *Early American fireplaces*, New York, 1977.
Lehnemann, W., *Eisenöfen*, Munich, 1984.
Lindsay, J. Seymour, *Iron and brass implements of the English and American house* (repr. ed.), London, 1970. An important reference work about the multifarious objects used in the home including fire irons, cooking implements and lighting.
Lloyd, N., 'Domestic ironwork. I. Firebacks', *Archaeologival Review*, LVIII, 1925.
Mainwaring-Baines, J., *Wealden firebacks*, Hastings, 1958. One of the few surveys of firebacks in print. Useful.
Mercer, Henry C., *The bible in iron* (repr. ed.), Doylestown, Pennsylvania, 1961.
Schroeder, Albert, *Deutsche öfenplatten*, Leipzig, 1936. German stove-plates discussed and illustrated.
Sotheby, London, Belgravia, *Great stove vent, cast iron decorative heating and cooking stoves*, 7 March 1979.
Vermeersch, Valentin, *Cuisines anciennes*, Bruges, 1992.
Wilhide, Elizabeth, *The fireplace*, Boston and London, 1994.
Wright, Lawrence, *Home fires burning: The history of domestic heating and cooking*, London, 1964.

Iron for Lighting

Bourne, J., and Brett, V., *Lighting in the domestic interior*, London, 1992.
Country house lighting, 1660-1890, Leeds City Art Galleries. 1992 exhibition catalogue.
D'Allemagne, Henry-René, *Histoire du luminaire*, Paris, 1891. Copiously illustrated.
Hayward, Aurthur H., *Colonial lighting*, Boston, 1923.
Henriot, G., *Encyclopédie du luminaire, formes et décors apparentes depuis l'antiquité jusq'en 1870*, Paris, 1933.
Janneau, G., *Le luminaire...art deco licht-objekte*, Stuttgart, 1991. Art Deco lighting designs drawn from Art Deco exhibitions. Multi-lingual.
Laing. Alastair, *Lighting*, London, 1982.
Mazil, Nadja, *American lighting, 1840-1940*, Atglen, PA, 1995.

Iron for Furniture

Aslin, E., 'The Iron Age of furniture', *Country Life*, October 1963.
Anon, 'French 18th-century iron furniture', *Connaissance des arts*, No. 68, October, 1957.
Hayward, J. F., 'A chair for the Kunstkammer of the Emperor Rudolf II', *Burlington*, 122, 1980.
Himmelheber, Georg, *Möbel aus eisen*, Munich. 1996.
—- 'The beginnings of cast iron garden furniture production', in *Cast iron from Central Europe, 1800-50*. Exhibition at Bard Center, New York, 1994.
—- *Cast iron furniture and other furniture*, London, 1996.
Ostergard, D. E., ed., *Bent wood and metal furniture, 1850-1946*, Washington DC, 1987.
Wilson, D. M., 'An inlaid iron folding stool in the British Museum', *Medieval Archaeology*, vol. I, 1957.

Iron and Security

Blair, C., 'The most superb of all royal locks', *Apollo*, December, 1966.
D'Allemagne, H., *Les anciens maitres serruriers et leurs meilleurs travaux*, Paris, 1943.
Eames, P., 'Medieval furniture', *Furniture History Society Journal*, XIII, 1977.
Eras, Vincent, *Locks and keys throughout the ages*, Dordrecht, 1957.
Jennings, Celia, *Early chests in wood and iron*, London, 1974.
Mandel, Gabriele, *Clefs*, Paris, 1992. Very thorough and good photos.
Monk, Eric, *Locks and keys, their history and collection*, Aylesbury, 1974.
Penny, W. E. W., 'The art of the locksmith', *Connoisseur*, VII, 1903, ptII, pp.208-12.
—- 'The medieval keys in Salisbury Museum', *Connoisseur*, vol. XXIX, January 1911.
Prade, C., *Musée Bricard: Musée de la Serrure, Guide*, Paris, 1986.
Roe, F., *Ancient church chests and chairs*, London, 1929.

Vaudour, C., *Clefs et serrures des origines au commencement de la Renaissance, catalogue du Musée Le Secq des Tournelles*, pt. 2, Rouen, 1980.

Iron and the Church
See Part 1 also.

Baur-Heinhold, M., *Schmiedeeisen grabkreuze*, Munich, 1984.
Cox, J. C., *English church fittings, furniture and accessories*, London, 1923.
Victorian church art, Victoria & Albert Museum, London, 1971. Exhibition catalogue.
Vrooman, Nicholas, and Marvis, P. A,. eds, *Iron spirits*, Fargo, N. Dakota, 1982.

Small-scale Ironwork

Fennimore, D., 'Tobacco boxes', *Antique Metalware Society*, 3, 1995.
Gentle, R., and Feidl, *Domestic metalwork, 1640-1820*, London, 1994.
Glissman, A. H., *The evolution of the sad-iron*, California, 1970.
Vincent, Clare, 'Precious objects in iron', *Metropolitan Museum of Art Bulletin*, 22, 1964.

Jewellery

Jewellery in Europe and America, new times, new thinking, London, Crafts Council, 1996.
Clifford, A., *Cut steel and Berlin iron jewellery*, London, 1971.
Phillips, C., *Jewelry from antiquity to the present*, London, 1995.

PART 3: IRONWORKING PRODUCTION, TECHNIQUES AND GLOSSARY

Techniques, Technology and Conservation

Ashurst, John and Nicola, *Practical building conservation*, vol. 4: *Metals*, London, 1988.
Cleere, H., and Crossley, D., *The iron industry of the Weald*, Leicester, 1985.
Gale, W. K. V., *Ironworking*, Tring, 1981. Clear account by a practitioner for the non-specialist.
Haedeke, Hanns-Ulrich, *Metalwork*, London and New York, 1970.
Tweedale, Geoffrey, *Giants of Sheffield steel*, Sheffield, 1986.
Tylecote, R. F., *A history of metallurgy*, London, 1976. A detailed and scholarly account of the technology of iron.
Untracht, Oppi, *Metal techniques for craftsmen*, London and New York, 1968. Useful practical guide, well illustrated.

Colour

Baty Patrick, 'Palette of the past', *Country Life*, 3 September 1992.
Bridgwater, D., 'Finishes on cast iron', *Official Architect*, May 1945.
Hawkes, Pamela W., 'Paints for architectural cast iron', *APT Bulletin* (USA), vol. XI, 1979.
Paint and its part in architecture, Jenson and Nicholson Ltd, 1930.

SOURCES OF INFORMATION
Some museums will advise, otherwise:

British Artist Blacksmiths Association
Chris Topp, General Secretary
Syndhurst, Carlton Husthwaite, Thirsk, N.Yorks Y07 2BJ.

British Cast Iron Research Association
Bordesley Hall, Alvechurch, Birmingham B48 7QH.

Conservation Unit, Museums and Galleries Commission
16 Queen Anne's Gate, London SW1H 9AA.
Advice on finding and employing a conservator.

The Crafts Council of Great Britain
44 Pentonville Road, London N1.
Has a register of contemporary makers, also conservators.

Ornamental Smiths' Workshop
English Heritage, c/o Keysign House, 429 Oxford Street, London W1R 2HD.
Advice on how to proceed with repairs.

Rural Development Commission
Paul Allen, Forgework Advisor
141 Castle Street, Salisbury, Wilts.

The Society for the Protection of Ancient Buildings
37 Spital Square, London E1 6DY.
Advice on building history and structural repairs.

MUSEUMS WITH IRONWORK

A selection of those with good or important, often specialist collections of ironwork, or with technical displays. Those indicated * have particularly outstanding collections. Those indicated † also contain collections of designs, or have libraries with relevant books and catalogues. An appointment to visit is essential, as larger items are often kept in distant stores.

AUSTRIA

Vienna Museum of Applied Arts

BELGIUM

Bruges Gruuthusemuseum
Brussels Musées Royaux d'Art et d'Histoire

DENMARK

Copenhagen National Museum

FRANCE

Avignon *Musée Bricard
            Musée Calvet
Jarville Musée de l'Art de Fer
Nancy Musée Lorrain
Paris †Musée Carnavalet
         Musée de Cluny
         †Musée des Arts Decoratifs
         Musée National des Arts et Traditions Populaires
Rouen Musée le Secq des Tournelles
Strasbourg Musée des Arts Decoratifs

GERMANY

Berlin Berlin Museum
Dresden Historisches Museum
Frankfurt Museum für Kunsthandwerk
Munich Bayerisches Nationalmuseum
Nuremberg Germanisches Nationalmuseum

GREAT BRITAIN

Amberley, W. Sussex Chalk Pits Museum
Cambridge Cambridge and County Folk Museum
Cardiff Welsh Folk Museum, St Fagan's
Dartford, Kent Brooking Collection, University of Greenwich
Edinburgh National Museum of Scotland
Falkirk †Falkirk Museum
Guildford Guildford Museum
Hastings Hastings Museum and Art Gallery
Lewes, E. Sussex Anne of Cleves House Museum

London Museum of London
          †Science Museum
          *†Victoria and Albert Museum
Reading Museum of English Rural Life, Reading University
Telford, Salop *†Ironbridge Gorge Museum
York Castle Museum

ITALY

Milan Museo Nazionale della Scienza e della Tecnica

NORWAY

Oslo Norsk Folkemuseum, Bygdoy

RUSSIA

St Petersburg The Hermitage

SPAIN

Vich Museo Arqueológico Artistico Episcopal

SWEDEN

Lund Kulturhistoriska Museet
Stockholm Nordiska Museet
             Statens Historiska Museet

SWITZERLAND

Basle Historisches Museum
Geneva Musée d'Art et d'Histoire
Zurich Schweizerisches Landesmuseum

UNITED STATES

Albany, New York Albany Institute of History and Art
Birmingham, Alabama Birmingham Museum of Art
Carbondale, Illinois Southern Illinois University
Chicago Art Institute of Chicago
Doylestown, Pennsylvania Mercer Museum and Bucks County Historical Society
Landis Valley, Pennsylvania The Pennsylvania Farm Museum
New York City The Metropolitan Museum of Art (including The Cloisters)
                 †Cooper-Hewitt National Design Museum, Smithsonian Institute
Philadelphia Philadelphia Museum of Art
St Louis St Louis Art Museum
Williamsburg, Virginia The Colonial Williamsburg Foundation
Winterthur, Delaware †Winterthur

INDEX

ACKNOWLEDGEMENTS

In writing a book that covers so wide a field, I am indebted to the work of many other individuals and institutions, especially to the fine resources of the Courtauld Institute of Art (Conway Library), the Cooper-Hewitt Library, New York, and the Winterthur Museum Library and Archive. Friends, family and colleagues have likewise contributed much, especially those who worked with me on redisplaying the western wing of the V&A's Ironwork Gallery in 1994: Sally Dormer, Sophie Lee, Anthony North, Pippa Shirley and Eric Turner. In the Museum I received generous encouragement and support from Mary Butler, Head of Publications, Philippa Glanville, Head of Metalwork, and Paul Greenhalgh, Head of Research. Particular thanks are due to Miranda Harrison and colleagues of V&A Publications for their care in seeing the book through the press, to the editor Moira Johnston and to Lynne Cope, who immaculately typed the final draft. For the visual appearance of the book I am especially indebted to the skill of the designer Bernard Higton, as well as to the particular generosity of the photographers John Gay, Anthony Kersting and Rosalind Solomon. The Museum photographers, especially Ken Jackson and Dominic Naish, capably bore a heavy burden uncomplainingly, and I am grateful too to Louise Hofman and Tamsin Daniel for organizing this. For assistance of many sorts my thanks go also to: Claude Blair, Barbara Drake Boehm, Christopher Brown, Louise and Helen Campbell, Charlotte Cotton, John Davis, Godfrey Evans, Renate Eikelmann, Donald Fennimore, Gilles Grandjean, Tammis Groft, Mark Haworth Booth, Erla Hohler, Briony Hudson, John and Betty Hyman, Betty Monkman, A. V. B. Norman, Bernard Nurse, James Oliver, Lorenz Seelig, T. J. Sloane, Peter Ross, Madeleine Tilley, Clare Vincent, Clive Wainwright, Philip Ward-Jackson, Jean-Pierre Willesme and Matthew Winterbottom. Most especial thanks go to my husband, for his patience and his hawk-eyed proof-reading.